THE
EXPEDITION

TRUE STORY OF THE FIRST HUMAN-POWERED
CIRCUMNAVIGATION OF THE EARTH

1 DARK WATERS

JASON LEWIS

BILLYFISH

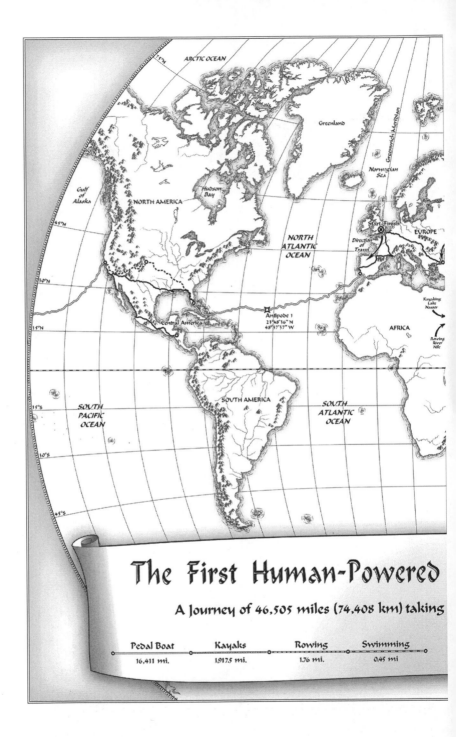

ARCTIC OCEAN

Greenland

Greenwich Meridian

Norwegian
Sea

Gulf
of
Alaska

Hudson
Bay

NORTH AMERICA

EUROPE

Start-Finish

NORTH
ATLANTIC
OCEAN

Direction
of
Travel

45°N

30°N

Kayaking
Lake
Nasser

15°N

Antipode 1
23°48'36" N
48°37'37" W

Central America

AFRICA

Rowing
River
Nile

SOUTH AMERICA

15°S

SOUTH
PACIFIC
OCEAN

SOUTH
ATLANTIC
OCEAN

30°S

45°S

The First Human-Powered

A Journey of 46,505 miles (74,408 km) taking

Pedal Boat	Kayaks	Rowing	Swimming
16,411 mi.	1,917.5 mi.	1.76 mi.	0.45 mi

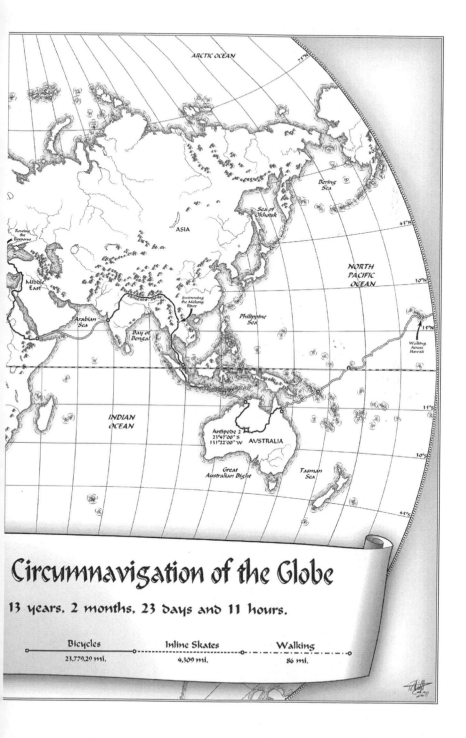

Circumnavigation of the Globe

13 years, 2 months, 23 days and 11 hours.

Bicycles	Inline Skates	Walking
23,779.29 mi.	4,309 mi.	86 mi.

First BillyFish Books edition 2012

For permission requests, write to the publisher: permissions@billyfishbooks.com
www.billyfishbooks.com

ISBN 978-0-9849155-0-7 (pbk.)

British Library Cataloguing in Publication Data. A catalogue record for this book is available
from the British Library.

Publisher's Cataloging-in-Publication data
Lewis, Jason, 1967-.
Dark waters : true story of the first human-powered circumnavigation of the earth / Jason
Lewis.
p. cm.
ISBN 978-0-9849155-0-7
Series : The Expedition.
1. Lewis, Jason, 1967 - --Travel. 2. Adventure travel. 3. Voyages and travels. 4. Voyages
around the world. 5. Human powered vehicles. 6. Spirituality. I. Title. II. Series.
G465 .L495 2012
910.4 --dc23   2012902555

All wood product components used in print versions of this book meet Sustainable Forestry
Initiative® (SFI®) Certified Sourcing (USA) and Forest Stewardship Council™ (FSC®)
Mixed Credit (UK) standards.

Cover photograph © Kenny Brown
Maps © Rob Antonishen/Cartocopia
Cover design by *the*BookDesigners

10 9 8 7 6 5 4 3 2 1

Contents

To my father, SEBERT LEWIS
1931 - 2011
From Mud, Through Blood to the Green Fields Beyond
you were always at my shoulder

There's a race of men that don't fit in,
A race that can't stay still;
So they break the hearts of kith and kin,
And they roam the world at will.
They range the field and they rove the flood,
And they climb the mountain's crest;
Theirs is the curse of the gypsy blood,
And they don't know how to rest.
—ROBERT W. SERVICE, *The Men That Don't Fit In*

"Where are the men?" the little prince at last took up the conversation again. "It is a little lonely in the desert..."
"It is also lonely among men," the snake said.
—ANTIONE DE SAINT-EXUPÉRY, *The Little Prince*

ROUNDING THE SOUTHERN EDGE of Lookout Point, I felt the hairs on the back of my neck stand up, like when you know you're being watched.

I glanced behind.

Two lidless eyes and a snub nose, gliding behind my kayak.

Fear gripped me instantly. Not the jittery type like when you come across a large spider in the bath. But the primal, fundamentally hard-wired horror of being hunted, considered prey. And the last fifty yards to shore, which should have been a winding down and quiet reflection on the entire Pacific crossing, instead became an adrenaline charged eruption of pumping arms and hammering heartbeat.

If it takes me in the water, I thought, *I'm finished…*

I tore frantically at the surface, snatching occasional glimpses behind. The predator was gaining easily.

My paddle blade touched sand. In a single movement, I yanked the Velcro fastenings on the spray-skirt, sprang from the cockpit, and spun to face my pursuer.

Nothing.

It was gone.

My blistered and swollen hands were shaking, stomach churning.

Shock. Yes, it must be shock kicking in…

Twenty-two miles was also a fair distance to paddle in five and a half hours, and a leak in the canvas hull had obliged frequent bailing. The sun played its part, too, radiating with savage ferocity from the mirrored surface of the Coral Sea, sapping every ounce from over-stretched, protesting muscles.

For now, though, I was safe on the beach, as long as daylight held.

I dumped the first load at the high tide mark—double-bladed wooden paddle, spray-skirt, and waterproof bags—turned to get another load, and froze.

At fifteen feet long, the way the thing bored through the slashing surf resembled a giant battering ram lathered in black pitch, brought to life by some abominable spell. With unswerving intent, the reptile swaggered towards my kayak parked at the water's edge, the monster in a low budget horror movie that just keeps coming.

I snatched the paddle and started running towards the water. What I would do when I got there I had no idea. I just knew my water, food, and satellite phone were about to be dragged out to sea. That would be it. Game Over.

This was a remote stretch of Queensland's northeast seaboard, 120 miles north of Cooktown, the last coastal settlement on the Cape York Peninsula before Papua New Guinea, four hundred miles to the north. I was well aware estuarine crocodiles populated these waters. It was hard not to be. Every other sentence out of a local's mouth had a croc in it.

"There's some big lizards out there mate," an aboriginal guide, Russell Butler, told me earlier in the day setting out from the beach at the Lizard Island Research Centre. "Watch yourself, orright?!"

The chance meeting already seemed a lifetime ago. As I ran, an eighties disco anthem I'd been humming that afternoon began looping in my head.

"Last night a deejay saved my life...
Last night a deejay saved my life from a broken heart."

My head often played tricks like this when the shit hit the fan. Black, sadistic humour, pretending everything was okay, situation normal. A defence mechanism to allow a person to keep functioning.

Nearing my boat, the croc was just yards away on the opposite side. Huge. Not so much the length as the width, a good four feet at the midriff, dark oblong scales forming a pattern of raised armour on the topside, merging to a smooth cream underbelly.

Using the hull as a protective shield, I reached over with my paddle and prodded its snout.

"Shoo, go on now, bugger off..."

The reptile responded by opening its mouth, revealing rows of ragged teeth set porcelain-white against a cavernous backdrop. It expelled a low hiss.

Up until now, the creature only appeared to have an issue with my kayak. That was about to change. Tail raised, mouth ajar, the croc lunged towards me. At the same time I stabbed. Gin trap jaws snapped over the paddle blade.*

A tug of war ensued. The harder I pulled, the tighter its grip. At 1,500 pounds, the animal only had to flick its head and the paddle would be torn from my hands. In desperation, I thrust away from me, into its throat. The blade came free. Then I swung it as hard as I could. A sharp splintering of wood, and I found myself holding the fractured end.

Shit!

Maybe I'd actually hit the eye like I was aiming for. Or, after five attempts at crossing the Pacific, enduring 8,320 miles of gale force winds, monstrous seas, blood poisoning, insanity, and countercurrents sweeping me back for weeks at a time, the sea gods had decided enough was enough.

The croc turned and slipped back into deeper water.

Adrenaline surged and my belly heaved.

I threw up.

"GET OFF THE beach *now*," the voice commanded urgently. I'd retrieved my satellite phone from the rear compartment of the kayak, and called my Aussie outback expert in Cairns, John Andrews. "They're bastards, wily as hell. They can't climb, though. You're best off looking for higher ground. If you camp on the beach, it'll wait until you're asleep. Then it'll come 'n getcha."

He wasn't exaggerating. A few months earlier, a family had been camping less than a hundred miles to the northwest in Bathurst Bay. In the early hours of the morning, thirty-four-year-old Andrew Kerr found himself being dragged from his tent—pitched thirty yards from

---

* Since hunting was banned in 1974, the "saltie" population in Australia has made a spectacular recovery, particularly in the northern part of the country where fewer people live. Competition for territory has risen accordingly, and my kayak, being roughly the same size and shape as a young male, was likely mistaken for an intruder by the dominant male of the area.

the water's edge—by a fourteen-foot saltie. Alicia Sorohan, a sixty-year-old grandmother, leapt onto the animal's back, forcing it to release. The crocodile then turned on her, breaking her nose and arm. Fortunately, her son arrived on the scene and dispatched it with a revolver—something I didn't have.

It was dark by the time I hobbled with the last of my gear up the steep, narrow path to the top of the headland. My feet were swollen. Like an idiot, I'd left my sandals on Bob and Tanya Lamb's porch. I slumped in the windswept grass, utterly spent, head lolling against a leathery tussock. The Southeast Trade Winds hushed to a whisper, and droves of mosquitoes appeared from nowhere, zinging in my ears. That was fine. I had no intention of sleeping. Far below, glowing orange in the beam of my headlamp, a pair of sleepless eyes patrolled back and forth.

I reached for my Ocean Ring. It was safe, on my left ring finger. I remembered the day I first put it on outside the Golden Gate Bridge, and the pledge I'd made to the sea: *From now on, we are one...* Had it worked? Perhaps. The Pacific, after all, had finally let me pass.

I cast further back, squinting into the depths of the Southern Hemisphere night, trying to recollect... How did I get to be stranded 25,000 miles from home, at the top of some godforsaken cliff, man-eater at the bottom, being bitten to death by mosquitoes in the first place?

PARIS
THE BIG IDEA

Most humans ... have settled for a life of mediocrity, days of despair and nights of tears. They are no more than living deaths confined to cemeteries of their choice.

—OG MANDINO, *The Greatest Miracle in the World*

Thirteen years earlier. Paris, August 1992

IT'S INCREDIBLE ISN'T IT," Steve exclaimed, "how no one's thought of it?" As he'd already pointed out, the world had been circumnavigated using everything from sailboats, to airplanes, to hot air balloons. Yet the purest, most ecologically sound method of all and doable for centuries, without using fossil fuels, was still up for grabs. "It'll be an original first, I'm sure of it!" he continued excitedly.

My old college pal Steve Smith and I were slumped on the kitchen floor of his flat in Paris, drinking Kronenbourg 1664 at two in the morning. A map of the world lay between us, paddled by the slowly revolving shadow of an ornate ceiling fan that gave the apartment an air of French colonial panache.

"So, you reckon all the other big firsts in exploration and adventure have been done?" I asked.

Steve had done his homework, proceeding to reel off some of the more notable feats of the last century: Amundsen beating Scott to the South Pole in 1911; Hillary and Norgay summiting Everest in 1953; Armstrong setting foot on the moon in 1969. By 1992, however, it was slim pickings with the exception of the deep oceans and outer space. Nearly every square inch of the planet's surface had been trampled upon, sailed across, flown, or driven over. Explorers and adventurers were fast becoming a rare breed, increasingly reliant upon inventive wordage to pass off a gimmick, or variation on a well-worn theme, as something genuinely different.

"It won't be long before the media," he finished off dryly, "run a story about the first blind-folded transsexual to snowboard down Everest in a thong."

I smiled. "That's been done already hasn't it?"

"Not on a dustbin lid."

Earlier that afternoon I'd flown from London, taking up Steve's invitation for "a bit of piss up—you know, just like old times." I should have smelt a rat right there. We'd barely seen each other since our final year at university. Why the grand reunion now all of a sudden?

The reason soon became clear after we rendezvoused at Charles de Gaulle Airport, and began lurching our way into the centre of the city on the metro. Clutching the steel bar above his head and raising his voice over the clattering wheels, Steve pitched the most ingenious, hare-brained, inspirational, irresponsible, guaranteed-to-give-your-mother-a-cardiac-arrest idea I had ever heard:

A human-powered circumnavigation of the globe...

Those few words hung suspended in the carriage for a moment, like a spell, putting goose bumps on my skin. I mean... to travel as far as you can go over land and sea, to the very ends of the Earth itself, under your own steam. No motors or sails. Just the power of the human body to get you there and back again. It had to be the ultimate human challenge.

As Steve continued outlining his plan, my head filled with wildly romantic images: riding bicycles across the barren steppes of Central Asia, trekking through the frozen wastes of the Himalayas, staring into the flames of a roaring campfire after a hard day hacking through the Amazonian rainforest. *What about the oceans?* I wondered. Rowing? Swimming? Paddling a Boogie Board? And why was Steve asking me of all people to join him?

I had absolutely no experience as a so-called "adventurer." I'd travelled before, but never far off the beaten track: Kenya for three months after school, Cyprus during college, and the US for a spell immediately afterwards. From the age of sixteen, I devoted myself to singing in a grunge band that played in all the usual London toilets: the Falcon in Camden, the Half Moon in Putney, the Bull and Gate in Kentish Town. It was fun in the early days when we hadn't taken ourselves too seriously. The first outfit, *Dougal Goes to Norway*, was a cover band distinguishable from the rest only by our Viking helmets and kilts—nothing on underneath. Later, we tried to make a proper go of it, releasing a vinyl EP. But with the entire band of five, plus two dogs and three cats, crammed in a two bedroom semi-detached house in Staines—The Shitehouse, as it was known—it had all become a bit of a grind.

I paid for my music habit with "Ballistic Cleaning Services Inc.," a window cleaning business under contract with various restaurants and hotels in the West London area. When not leaning off ladders buffing windows, my partner Graham and I could typically be found wheezing up and down the A332 between Egham and Bracknell in the pride of the fleet, an X-reg Morris Marina van costing fifty quid from a scrap yard off the Old Kent Road. Spray-painted with the slogan *"Get Realistic. Go Ballistic!"* the company jalopy had no registration, road tax certificate, or insurance. But it was mechanically sound. And apart from one occasion when a rear wheel fell off and overtook us along Ascot High Street, it had never let us down.

Surely, however, these weren't suitable qualifications for an undertaking such as this?

I shot Steve a sidelong look. "You *sure* you want me as your expedition partner?"

He nodded.

"And it'll take around three years to complete you say?"

"If we can find sponsorship."

Taking a swig, I surveyed my old friend. Like many of our desk-bound graduate peers, he looked anaemic, badly in need of some sun. But while others were already turning paunches, Steve remained athletic and trim, not an extra ounce of fat on his body. And he still had the same steady cobalt gaze.

The first time we met I was supine on a stranger's bed in one of the halls of residence, my arm around a girl, the other around a bottle of vodka. As the party wore on, I became dimly aware of the bed's owner—Steve as it turned out—glaring at me from across the room.

Steve took an instant dislike to "that unruly farm boy" who'd soaked his bed in vodka. In time, however, attending the same biology and geography lectures, we became good friends. After a weekend poaching trout on Dartmoor when we should have been sitting through stultifying lectures on tor formation at a local field studies centre, we began taking off on spontaneous rambles around London. A three-day hike on the Chilterns in south Oxfordshire was one. Disembarking the train at Princes Risborough, we discovered neither of us had a sleeping bag, or a tent. It was the middle of January. Night-time temperatures were well below freezing. That first night we slept on the floor of a pub, sneaking back through the lavatory window we'd left ajar before being turfed out. The second night we lucked out, chancing upon a hay barn. Otherwise, we would have likely frozen to death.

Such was our early friendship, defined by episodes of kamikaze impetuousness swaggering along the knife-edge of fate—the sharper the edge the better.

Further fuelled by beer, brainlessness and a shared bent for challenging authority, we developed a penchant for egging each other on in a series of puerile college pranks, culminating in the erection of a fifteen-foot-high penis made from cardboard, party balloons and a pink bed sheet on an ornate spire at the entrance to campus. The pathetically limp protest directed at a visiting politician, made even more so by a light drizzle, was the best we could deliver as an anti-establishment statement at the time.

Then we went our separate ways: Steve into a career as an environmental scientist, myself into the giddy world of crooning in dive bars and cleaning windows.

"So where did you get the idea?" I asked.

Steve pursed his lips and shook his head at the memory. "I was working for the OECD at the time.* At first I thought I'd be making

---

* The Organization for Economic Cooperation and Development.

a difference, writing reports for politicians to integrate environmental sustainability into their economic development policies."

Like a growing number in his field, Steve was alarmed by the ballooning number of human beings on the planet, ten billion by 2050, all aspiring to the same level of prosperity as the average Westerner—*as seen on TV*. Conservative estimates for meeting consumption demands without further depleting resources or biodiversity from 1994 levels was set at eight additional Earths.

"But the reports fell on deaf ears," he went on. "A habitable planet for future generations is a lovely idea, the economists said, but we simply can't afford it."

Instead of falling into line with offers of promotion and salary increases, Steve took a stand.

"I felt like grabbing those short-term-thinking fuckwits by their starched collars and saying, 'haven't you *seen* the data on climate trends and species extinctions? We can't afford *not* to do something. We'll be next!'"

Small wonder he was duly assigned to a very different field of study: assessing the environmental impact of creosote on motorway fence posts. Their plan worked. Steve became disillusioned, staring out of the window, his mind wandering…

"That's when I thought, what if I were free to do anything, *anything* at all, what would I be doing with my life right now?

He knew it had to be something to do with travel, and adventure, and on a big scale.

"And what bigger than around the world?"

The mode of propulsion was a stumbling block. It needed to be inexpensive, with minimal harm to the environment.

"Engines and I don't get along. And if animals were involved, they'd all be dead within the month."

Then it came to him. The Eureka Moment. The cheapest, least

technical, lowest impact power of all. Human power.

"So, what do you think Jase? You up for it?"

I looked out through the kitchen window, past the wrought-iron balcony into the Paris night. The blank spaces on the map with no roads or towns marked I found utterly captivating. And a sabbatical from music might revitalize the songwriting juices. Moreover, if we left sooner rather than later, I might avoid a thorny court case for crashing the Ballistic cleaning van into a Rolls Royce off the Fulham Road and having to do a runner.

But there was something else.

I cast my mind back to when I was sixteen, sitting in the warm, dusty office of the school's career advisor.

"What profession interests you?" he'd enquired.

"Why?" I answered.

"Why what?"

"Why a career?"

The advisor stared at me. "It's what people do. To earn a living."

"Right. But what's the endgame? The *point* of it?"

Put another way, I might have asked whether it was just about 'the job, the family, the fucking big television, the washing machine, the car, the compact disc player, the electronic tin opener, good health, low cholesterol, dental insurance, mortgage starter home…'* Wasn't there more to life than this?

Apparently there wasn't, as the careers advisor sighed and sent me on my way.

My fear was blindly subscribing to the whims of an increasingly materialistic society, with its shallow mediocrity and hollow indulgences, offering no deeper meaning or purpose than the indiscriminate production and consumption of Stuff, the treadmill existence of human battery hens.

---

*   *Trainspotting* by Irvine Welsh.

The Industrial Revolution had produced impressive leaps in technological advancements, for the West in particular, improving people's quality of life beyond question—healthcare, economic well-being, education, and so on. But where were the corresponding ethical advancements? Where was the philosophical framework to give value and meaning to these improvements? Our uniquely large brains had created systems and machines to make life safer and easier, but that was as far as it went. Human existence, and thus technology, boiled down to acquisition of power and resources. The key to success involved manipulating, exploiting, and generally competing against one's fellow man and other species with Darwinian zeal, employing the very same qualities that won us pole position in nature's league table in the first place.

But if Darwin was right, and natural selection is the blind chauffeur behind the wheel of evolution, driving human existence with no set route or destination in mind, why did people demand something "other" to give meaning to their lives? Like turning to a god, or some other invisible force pulling the strings according to a more intelligent design, providing them with a moral compass and higher purpose.

Life. How to live it?

Years after meeting with the career advisor, this still seemed to me the question that needed answering before any other, certainly before what cookie-cutter career to pick from the corporate vending machine. In a twenty-first century world imperilled by the myopic attitude of humans, the search for a unifying Philosophy for Life, one that offered a big picture perspective on how to live sustainably on a crowded planet, was a quest worthy of the dangers that lay ahead.

"Okay, I'll do it," I said.

Steve grinned. "Great!"

"There is, however, one other question I have before signing on the dotted line." I stabbed at the Atlantic and Pacific oceans on the map. "These blue areas—"

"Yes! Yes! The big wet bits," he interrupted enthusiastically.

"Right, the um… big wet bits. How do we get across those then?"

"Easy. We'll kayak from Scotland to Greenland, across to Canada, and then—"

"You're crazy. Neither of us has kayaked before!"

"Oh shit, Jase. How hard can it be? I mean, all you gotta do is go like this, and we'll get there eventually." And with these reassuring words, he lurched to his feet and began whirling his arms around his head in the manner of a paddling kayaker.

I roared with laughter. "I was wrong. You're not crazy. You're fucking insane!"

Clearly, neither of us had any idea of what we were getting into. But, as we found ourselves reminding each other frequently from that point on, lack of experience isn't a good enough reason not to try. Besides, as the sagacious old comic strip character Hagar the Horrible once noted, "Ignorance is the Mother of all Adventure." And if I'd known what I was letting myself in for, I probably would have never agreed to join.

ENGLAND
RAISING THE DREAM

Nothing will ever be attempted if all possible objections must first be overcome.

—SAMUEL JOHNSON

One year later… Ardleigh reservoir, Suffolk

THE MORNING AIR WAS clear. A stiff northeasterly blew unchallenged across the Broads from the North Sea, slicing to the bone through our meagre wool jerseys. We'd been at the reservoir since dawn, waiting for the boat builders to arrive with the recently completed hull. Today was a big day. By the end of it, we would know two things: whether the strange-looking contraption floated, and whether a customized propeller could move it through the water.

Chris had called the night before to say they'd run into a few technical difficulties. The trailer lights had died in the middle of Bridport, about the time they'd worked out that eight pounds between them wasn't near enough to buy fuel for the 275-mile journey to Suffolk. Towing a three-tonne trailer plus the hull, Hugo's long wheelbase Land Rover made eight miles to the gallon at best.

"Lucky we pulled off the road outside the Toll House pub," chuckled Chris, sounding happy at the turn of events. "The landlord's given us a lock-in, and bitter's only eighty-eight pence! Oh yeah, and we're calling round to see if anyone's got an AA card—"

The line went dead. Whether cheap booze or the Automobile Association amounted to a solution would remain a mystery until they showed up—if indeed they ever did.

It had been a busy year since meeting up in Paris. In the spring, Steve had left his job to begin planning the expedition full-time. Four months later, I followed suit by dissolving Ballistic Cleaning Services Inc., bringing to an end nearly a decade of pedigree cleaning care. To the great relief of our families, the idea to kayak from Scotland to Canada had been shelved early on. A call to the maritime museum in Exeter to enquire whether they knew of an ocean-going row boat for sale had produced a far more sensible way of crossing the big wet bits.

After listening to Steve's ambitious circumnavigation plans, the curator, a naval architect by trade, offered to design a human-powered vessel from scratch. Calling on his extensive knowledge of the twenty or so rowing boats that had crossed the Atlantic since 1896, some of which were displayed in the museum, Alan Boswell drew up the blueprints for a twenty-six-foot craft, powered by propeller, with enough storage space to sustain two people with food and provisions for up to 150 days without resupply.

"Another advantage of a pedal powered vessel," Alan wrote in a follow-up letter, *"is that since you will be cycling across continents, you will be fantastically fit for pedalling, but not for rowing, when you get to the ocean sections."*

Connecting with Alan had been the first in a series of lucky breaks, elevating the idea from drunken talk to at least drawing board status. David Goddard, the museum's founder and director, generously provided a storage shed for the boat's construction. The icing on the cake was reconnecting with my old childhood pal, Hugo Burnham, recently graduated from the prestigious wooden boatbuilding college at Lowestoft. Along with his friend Chris Tipper, also a newly qualified shipwright, we now had a relatively inexpensive way of building what commercial boatyards had quoted £26,000.

Further bolstered by the donation of otherwise pricey hardwood from the Ecological Trading Company, one of the few businesses in the country importing timber harvested only from sustainably managed sources, construction commenced. Four months later, a cold-molded hull, comprising strip cedar planks sealed with epoxy resin and overlaid with hardwood veneers, emerged from the workshop.

It was time to stick it in the water.

The Times and *The Daily Telegraph* had agreed to turn up and run picture stories, announcing our plans to the wider world for the first time. Publicity was all-important to secure the sponsorship needed to embark on the expedition proper.

BY TEN O'CLOCK, there was still no sign of Chris and Hugo. The two photographers were trading anxious glances, perhaps wondering if they were the unwitting victims of a prank by their picture desk editors: "I need you to drive to the Arse End of Nowhere and shoot a story about a couple of nutters planning to use a pedalo to go around the world. You know, one of those things they rent out for five quid an hour on the Serpentine Lake in Hyde Park. *Come in number ten, your time is up!*"

It certainly sounded like a hoax.

Just then, a flatbed lorry with orange flashing lights rumbled through the marina entrance, a creaking Land Rover lashed to the top. An equally dilapidated-looking trailer bore something resembling an oversized canoe, painted white. If it weren't for the Automobile Association stickers on the side of the cab you'd be forgiven for thinking the gypsies were in town.

The ramshackle procession ground to a halt and the driver's side door burst open, letting a waft of smoke billow out into the crisp morning sunlight. The driver emerged, looking wild-eyed and shaken, and staggered off in the direction of the public lavatories. Next came three characters stepping off the pages of a Fabulous Furry Freak Brothers comic book.* The leader was the spitting image of Freewheelin' Franklin, a pirate with crooked teeth, ponytail reaching down past his backside, and a two-prong waxed goatee dangling from his chin like the whiskers on a catfish. Fat Freddy followed, freckled, with a ginger Afro. The last of them, Phineas Freakears, was tall and lithe with a large rudder for a nose, and locks of dark hair hanging around his head like lampshade tassels.

Spotting Steve and me by the water's edge, the trio altered course in formation and floated towards us as if on a cloud. All of them were grinning like Cheshire Cats.

---

* Cartoon strip hippies from San Francisco with a talent for smoking vast quantities of marijuana and defying authority.

"Aarrr, yer mangy dogs!" roared the pirate.

"Thought you boys weren't going to make it," Steve replied tersely.

"'Course we'd bloody make it Smithers!" retorted Hugo. "Mainly thanks to good ol' Eddie here and his AA card."

The ginger Afro bobbed and grinned and strafed the air with a machine gun laugh. *"Hehehehehe!* Got a call from Chris just after midnight last night, asking if I'd kept up my AA membership. Next thing I knew we were all in the Toll House having a—*hehehehehe!*—lock-in, waiting for the recovery van to arrive."

"Bloody lucky," said Chris, alias Phineas, looking furtively over his shoulder to make sure the driver was out of earshot. "The AA guy twigged we didn't have any money for fuel, but we'd sprinkled some sugar around the petrol cap. Spun him a yarn about having an argument with some skinheads in the boozer. *Bastards must've poured sugar in the fuel tank after they got kicked out.* What could he do?"

"Worked bootifully!" boomed Hugo. "Couldn't start the motor could 'e? He'd blow it good 'n proper loik. Had to call for a flatbed."

Steve was now smiling, won over by the latest ingenuity that kept the expedition moving forward on financial fumes.

An hour later, the virgin hull slipped off the back of the trailer into the reservoir. Standing waist-deep on the boat ramp, Chris wrestled the one-inch stainless steel propeller shaft through the deep-sea seal leading into the hull. He then fastened a two-bladed, fifteen-inch aluminium propeller to the end.

Steve and I climbed gingerly aboard, the hull wobbling unnervingly. A fighter-pilot-style cockpit of polycarbonate windows served as a protective shell, at the rear of which a builder's breezeblock doubled as a seat. The propulsion system comprised the A-frame of a cannibalized bicycle flipped upside down and bolted to the keel. Both the crank arms and front sprocket remained attached. But instead of a back wheel, the chain powered an industrial gearbox turning the drive through ninety degrees. This, in turn, spun the propeller shaft.

Steering was like operating a sports kite. Two lengths of rope ran forward from the top of the rudder to a set of pulleys either side of the cabin. The pulleys turned the lines 180 degrees back to the pedaller, who pushed and pulled a pair of handles salvaged from an old angle grinder in alternate directions for port and starboard.

With the photographer from *The Times* perched on the roof, nervously clutching his camera, Steve lowered himself carefully onto the breezeblock, and pressed his bare feet to the pedals. There was a squeal of complaint. Then the boat moved forward, grudgingly. Only a few feet, but it moved. And we were still afloat.

The expedition now had sea legs.

WITH CHRIS AND Hugo working in Exeter, surviving on the dole and the proceeds of loose change thrown into a donations box outside their workshop, Steve and I based ourselves in London, also surviving on the dole, a target of endless abuse down the pub.

"What the bloody hell are you two thinking?" roared Lofty, our six-feet, six-inch Yorkshireman friend over a beer at The Dove in Hammersmith. Tears were streaming down his cheeks from laughing so hard. "I mean, thirty-five quid a week on the *Rock 'n Roll* isn't going to get you around the world now is it? Word of advice lads, forget the whole pea-brained idea."

Finally, as if disclosing classified information, he leaned forward and hissed, "Joost admit it, you two losers aren't going *anywhere*—apart from the bar that is. Now get the fookin' beers in!"

As a used car salesman buying old bangers for a pittance at South London car auctions and then flogging them for scandalous sums through the free ads paper *Loot*, Lofty wasn't one to talk about going anywhere, either.

But this was typical of the UK's home-grown brand of Tall Poppy Syndrome, a nationwide condition whereby anyone caught breaking ranks and trying to sneak their life off in a new direction was automatically branded a turncoat, a traitor. And heaven forbid they actually become successful. Convention called for people to keep their heads down in their little rut. If you tried to make a run for it, the mob would drag you down like a pack of wolves, back into the shit pit with them.

Secretly, it made us even more determined to prove them wrong.

A few people took the idea seriously, Steve's father being one. Stuart had the energy of a five-year-old trapped inside a fifty-five-year-old body. Raised in the George Muller orphanage in Bristol until the age of fifteen, he wore the grizzled mantle of a survivor, beaten into shape by the brutish conditions and regular thumpings of the bible. He quickly became a walking, talking evangelist for the expedition.

Perhaps inadvertently expressing a piece of his own wounded soul, Stuart had a remarkable talent for making a person feel genuinely needed, especially when it came to forking out the cash. His local pub, *The Prince Alfred* in Queensway, was a favourite early hunting ground. Introducing himself with a winning smile and tip of his leather Crocodile Dundee hat to a group of complete strangers, he could sweep aside the initial scepticism—on occasion, outright hostility—and within five minutes have them all eating out of his hand. Even during the embryonic stages when the expedition was still just a fantasy, his infectious enthusiasm regularly had customers handing over ten pounds for a vinyl name on a boat that didn't even exist yet.

This was the early seed money that helped purchase materials to start building the boat. Steve then set out to bicycle 1,700 miles from London to Marrakech, completing his goal in an impressive seventeen days, adding a further £3,250 of individual pledges to the pot. At the same time, a concerted letter-writing campaign to marine equipment manufacturers yielded a steady trickle of paints, resins, rope, polycarbonate windows, bilge pumps, watertight bulkheads, a compass, and so on. In return, we promised the ultimate in field-testing, and photographs of their products in action. Mars UK donated 4,000 Mars Bars. My father talked the British Army out of 250 MRE (meals ready to eat) ration packs.

Despite early successes with equipment, there was still the small matter of where £150,000, the budget for the entire project, would come from. Over the next twelve months, more than 300 tailored proposals were submitted to a wide range of prospective title sponsors, each one followed up persistently by phone. They were met with an equally persistent stream of rejections:

"It's a wonderful idea ... truly inspirational," read the response from a popular battery manufacturer. "Linking longevity to our brand is a perfect fit. However, the three years proposed for the event is a little too long even for one of our batteries!"

Translated as: *Hey guys, we'll all be pushing up daisies by the time you finish this thing...*

Or, one from a well-known insurance corporation:

"The opportunity of associating our company with your daring adventure is a little too risky for our sponsorship strategy at this time."

Translated as: *Watching your boat sink a mile out from shore on national television, with you guys wearing one of our shirts, will do little for customer confidence...*

More often than not, it was just a form letter:

"After careful consideration, we regret to inform..."

Translated as: *Bugger off you scroungers and get a job like everybody else...*

Even Richard Branson turned us down because, according to his PR people, "Richard would want to do this himself."

Translated as: *Just bugger off.*

Then, in early February, our prayers were answered. A £30,000 offer came through from Fyfe's Bananas to be a supporting sponsor.

With one backer in place, attracting others would be easy.

There was, however, a slight catch. The deal involved turning the boat into a giant banana, painted yellow, and pedalling our first ocean as "The Banana Boys."

It was too humiliating a prospect to consider seriously.

—————∞∞∞————

IT WAS THE spectacular indifference of the UK business community, patronage we'd naïvely assumed would be a shoe-in considering the Unique Selling Point on offer, which sowed the early seeds of demise with the boat builders. Steve was sending them as much money as he could. Even so, by Christmas, proper compensation for their efforts was looking no more likely than it had a year previously. Hugo and Chris were becoming understandably disgruntled, and relations were stretched to breaking point.

Our visits to help work on the boat didn't improve matters. As well as being ham-fisted with power tools, we unknowingly dragged them into working their weekends when all they really wanted was to be taken out to the pub and rewarded for their efforts.

Like the proud parents of an angelic child whom the rest of the world sees as an abomination demanding never-ending attention, Steve and I had fallen into the trap of assuming that everyone working on the project—which already bore the hallmarks of a Frankenstein monster—shared the same enthusiasm of working long hours and drawing unemployment to keep body and soul together.

Money troubles aside, in January Steve decided Hugo needed to be relieved of his role as support team leader, a position that involved transporting a camera crew and supplies through the wilds of Siberia. The boat builder's fierce independence, natural distrust of authority, and caustic satire made for amusing repartee, but for occasions when everyone needed to be singing from the same hymn sheet, they were considered potential liabilities.

Steve and I drove down from London to the Marshwood Vale for a meeting with Hugo at The Bottle Inn, home of the world-famous nettle eating competition—an appropriate venue for the task at hand. Having known him since the age of five, I asked to be the one to break the grim news. Also, I knew of Hugo's particular dislike of Steve's self-styled leadership, and having been through similar ordeals letting band members go in years gone by, I knew it best to tell a person straight up, giving the reasons afterwards.

My request, however, was denied. As expedition leader, Steve wanted-ed to do it himself.

It was dark by the time we arrived. The public bar, with its low oak beams and smoke-stained ceiling, was near empty. We bought a round of Palmers IPA and planted ourselves on a pair of stools next to a roaring fire. Ten minutes later Hugo breezed in, ordered a pint, and took a stool opposite. The atmosphere bristled with tension. He knew something was up.

Steve began: "Is there anything about your attitude, or approach to being support team leader, you feel needs to change, Hugo?"

Oh no, I thought, *not a trick question. Just tell him he's off the team!*

Hugo cocked his head and twiddled his waxed moustache. "Err… nope." He looked nonplussed. "Can't think of anything."

Half an hour later, the meeting broke down, everyone bent out of shape. Poor old Hugo stormed off into the night, unsure of what was being asked of him. Steve was exasperated with Hugo for remaining stubborn enough not to submit to self-critique. I was furious with Steve for essentially trying to get Hugo to sack himself.

Would it have made a difference being more upfront? Who knows. Either way the result was the same, and the fallout horrendous. A childhood friendship between Hugo and me was forfeit. Our parents, who had known each other for decades, were forced to take sides. To cap it all, relations between Steve and I were badly strained, leaving the smouldering embers for future resentment to flare.

Chris was also put in a difficult position. Obliged by his friendship with Hugo to down tools, he was forced to make an impossible decision: show solidarity with his boat-building partner and walk off the job, or stand by his commitment to a project he felt proud to be a part of, and ultimately responsible to. Not least, because the very thing he and Hugo were creating, in a sense, defined it.

Fortunately for the expedition, he chose the latter. But it cost him a friendship too.

As WELL AS fallings-out, another feature of being continually broke planning an expedition was the need to learn a staggering array of new skills we couldn't afford to pay anyone else to do. This meant learning how to use a computer, no mean feat back in the days of MS DOS, writing proposals, press releases, public speaking, public relations, drawing up budgets (ever-hopefully), pitching to potential sponsors, applying for visas, researching route options, first aid training…

One thing beyond us, however, was how to film it. After two early camera operators fell by the wayside, a magical solution transpired from north of the border in the form of Kenny Brown, a native Glaswegian and budding documentary filmmaker. We met for a show-and-tell one March evening at the Chandos pub, north of Trafalgar Square. Steve and I couldn't understand a word Kenny said. The thick Scottish brogue firing off at a thousand words a minute proved utterly unfathomable:

*"Soonds loch an amazin' adventure ye tois haegot gonnae thur."**

"Uh, I'm sorry?"

---

* Sounds like an amazing adventure you two have got going there.

*"So when daeyetois think yoo'll beheadin' aff 'en?"**

"Eh? What was that again?"

He was an intriguing character to look at. A pointy nose, shaped like a turnip pulled out of the ground at an awkward angle, was set above a mouth too small for its head, the top of which was shaved entirely apart from a forelock of brown hair sprouting out like a proboscis. His eyes were shrewd and constantly moving, scrutinizing, suggesting a razor sharp mind at work.

Being at a loss to understand a single word he was saying, the proboscis transfixed me instead. Occasionally, when he leaned forward for his beer, it slipped and dangled over his glass like some tubular sucking device. Fascinated as a child by the emergency stop cords on trains, it was all I could do not to reach out and give it a good yank to see what might happen.

Kenny worked part time as a bicycle messenger to supplement his filmmaking aspirations, and lived in a spartan North London squat with eleven others. His milky complexion was maintained by an exclusively vegan diet, upheld with strict Calvinist-like fervour along with a number of other austere opinions, not least a violent dislike of slackers, hippies, and anything remotely touchy-feely. As Steve began outlining our plans to interview schoolchildren along the way for a film on world citizenship—*"To encourage empathy, tolerance, and compassion between cultures"*—I noticed Kenny squirming in his seat. From what could be deciphered from the rapid-fire volleys, his main interest in the project was the biking, the filming and *"Taykin' phoo-oos."* Everything else was fluff.

Despite the language barrier and emotional allergies, Kenny's showreel was inspired, and his no-nonsense, can-do attitude clearly an asset. He was duly invited to join. A week later, I became the squat's thirteenth

---

* So when do you two think you'll be heading off then?

member, partly to concentrate on the media effort with Kenny, but also to create breathing space between Steve and I. We'd be living in each other's pockets for the next three years as it was. The last thing we wanted was to start the expedition needing a holiday from each other.

Encompassing four floors of a rambling Russell Square town house, the Guildford Street squat quickly became the nerve centre for the press campaign, filming, bike equipment, food, and other overland logistics. Though the place was functional, comfort was not a word to use in the same sentence to describe it. The walls and floors were stripped bare. There was no heating. During the freezing months of March and April, Kenny and I spent our days bundled up in every piece of clothing we owned, tapping away at a pair of prehistoric computers salvaged from a skip, writing sponsorship proposals until the early hours of the morning. Exhausted, we would then roll up on the floor and grab a few hours sleep.

Gulag-like conditions aside, the squat's other denizens yielded a veritable treasure trove of artists, authors, musicians, blaggers, and petty criminals. The Guildford Street Gang was always ready to lend a hand in the effort, in some cases becoming semi-permanent fixtures. There was Jim, a disc jockey and editor of the mordant political magazine *Squall*, who volunteered as the expedition's unpaid press officer; Catriona, a voluptuous redhead, whose adroit handle on English prose knocked our sponsorship proposals into shape; Fingers, an amateur boxer turned professional thief, who specialized in cheque fraud; and Martin, a mild-mannered vegetarian chef and skilled bike mechanic, who offered to set up our bicycles and assemble the food for the Atlantic crossing.

The combined effort produced a very different outcome to what otherwise might have been had the expedition actually managed to hook a title sponsor, as money, and the way it twists agendas, never came into it. At our first major press event on the River Thames, when the expedition's UK patron, HRH The Duke of Gloucester, christened the boat *Moksha*, the Guildford Street Gang expedited logistics.* The groundswell of an organic support network was a characteristic of the expedition that stuck early on, becoming central to its identity over the years. It kept the whole thing real, a human-powered expedition to its core.

BY MID-APRIL, *Moksha* was ready for a proper sea-trial. First, however, we needed to make sure she would automatically self-right in the event she capsized. Before taking her down to Salcombe, we took advantage of the hand-operated crane at the museum to flip her over in the River Exe. After an initial unmanned test roll, Kenny and I clambered inside the cabin and buckled up using seat belts reclaimed from the Ballistic Cleaning van. Kenny had borrowed a camera to film. Steve and Chris operated the crane.

As she tilted to ninety degrees, water began spewing in around the sliding hatch. My head was resting on the plywood roof, hair swimming in a rising pool of water.

"You okay Kenny?" I shouted, watching the proboscis flip upside down.

"Yeah. This seat's comin' apart, tho."

The water was up to my eyes. "Jesus!"

Then, a gut-wrenching spin—"*Woooooaaaahhh!*"—and we were suddenly upright again, torrents of water cascading everywhere.

What happened next was one of the most humiliating episodes in the entire expedition. Having benefited so greatly from the loan of the

---

*   Moksha is a Sanskrit word meaning freedom, or liberation, from all worldly desires, ignorance, and suffering. For Hindus and Buddhists, it represents the last state of transcendence before nirvana, the final release from Samsara, the cycle of death and rebirth (reincarnation). The choice of name was inspired by Aldous Huxley's book, *Island*.

workshop, we'd decided to stage a media event to raise publicity for the museum, which was struggling to avoid closure.

The idea was to pedal *Moksha* around the sheltered canal basin, letting press photographers snap the world's first two-man ocean pedal boat going through her paces, and then wrap up with interviews.

Chris Court from the Press Association was there on the dockside. He was joined by a carrot-headed journalist claiming to be from *Yachting Monthly*, and several other reporters from local papers. The next evening, when we pedalled out of Salcombe estuary to spend our first night at sea, one of the *Sky Sports* television channels would run a live interview patched through from our newly installed VHF radio, running some of Kenny's pre-recorded footage in the background.

Cautiously, I pedalled out into the muddy-brown river, swollen and turbulent with recent rain. Steve stood in the cockpit posing for the cameras.

"Over here Steve. Give us a wave!" yelled the snapper from the *Western Daily News*.

"Can you turn the boat around and come towards me, please?" This was the *Dorset Evening Echo*.

Steve leaned his head into the cockpit. "Did you hear that Jase?"

"Yup, just give me a second." I shoved the rudder hard over.

Nothing happened. I tried pulling and pushing my hands in opposite directions, but there was still no response.

"Err... Jason..."

The current was turning the boat.

"We need to turn around, mate!"

"I—I can't! The rudder's jammed or something!" I tried pedalling backwards. It was hopeless.

The flood run-off was sweeping us sideways down the river, faster and faster, the water sloshing and gurgling all around. And now there was another sound, like low, rolling thunder.

"Jase!" shouted Steve. "There's a fucking waterfall!"

Pedalling like the clappers, the best I could do was head broadside to the current, aiming for a concrete wall bordering a builder's yard.

KERRRUUNNCH! The sickening sound of splintering wood echoed across the basin. *Moksha* was now drifting stern first, all control gone. Steve scrambled out onto the foredeck, frantically snatching at low-lying willow branches. Our disgrace was complete when a noisy black inflatable appeared and plucked us off the lip of the dam just in time. Blushing furiously, we were dragged back to the waiting line of journalists, all of them sucking on the ends of their pencils, trying desperately not to laugh.

The next morning an article appeared in *The Daily Star* tabloid, entitled: PEDAL SUB SUNK!

According to the *Yachting Monthly* reporter, in reality a scumbag hack who'd clearly never been anywhere near a sailboat in his life, '*A pedal powered submarine was swept out to sea by high winds … before capsizing and sinking*'.

As well as learning a lot about the nefarious workings of the press that day, we made our acquaintance with an essential feature of the operational workings of the boat. Steering depended entirely on something called a centreboard, that three-foot-long piece of timber we'd left behind in the workshop.

THE FOLLOWING AFTERNOON we re-launched *Moksha* into Salcombe harbour, loaded her with three days of provisions, and headed for the open sea—centreboard firmly in place this time.

For Steve, this was to be his first night at sea, ever. He had more experience of overland travel having ridden a bicycle more than a mile since leaving school. I had more experience of boats having actually been in one.

After pedalling for what seemed an eternity, the dark outline of Bolt Head refused to get any closer. We switched. Within minutes, Steve's face was clenched in similar frustration. It was mind-numbing stuff. We exchanged glances, and cracked up laughing.

"Fucking boring isn't it."

"To put it mildly."

"Look," I said, furthering our mutual cause. "We know this is going to be a nightmare once we get out on the Atlantic proper. So why prolong the agony?"

Steve nodded. "It's opening time in half an hour, too."

More sniggering, and by eight o'clock, thanks mainly to the incoming tide, we were back in the Kings Arms, warming up next to the fire with Stuart and Kenny.

Stuart raised his glass. "Well, here's to successful sea-trials, eh lads!"

"Aye, awl fifteen minutes o' them," Kenny muttered derisively.

The drinks flowed, and as the evening wore on, the heat of the fire and the drone of background chatter conspired and I found myself slipping into a soporific coma. But something in the back of my mind was needling away. Something crucial we'd forgotten.

At a quarter to eleven, I remembered what it was.

"Shit! Steve, the interview with Sky Sports!"

We leapt to our feet and dashed outside to the public phone box. Squeezing inside, Steve dialled the number from a scrap of paper while I rummaged for a ten pence coin.

We were just in time.

"Putting you straight through," the producer said brusquely. "You're on in ten seconds." In the background, we could hear the lacquered voice of a male presenter leading into the interview.

"…And now joining us on the line from the English Channel, we have Steve Smith and Jason Lewis preparing for their historic circumnavigation attempt with three days of sea-trials. Good evening gentlemen!"

"Hi there," replied Steve.

"So we're looking at some footage taken earlier today of you pedalling around Salcombe harbour. Water looks nice and calm. The conditions must be very different out at sea, right?"

My expedition partner squinted into the glass of the telephone box, but only his moon-like reflection loomed back. "Yeah. It's a bit windy…"

"Of course. And Jason, tell us what you had for dinner tonight."

My mind went blank.

Steve grabbed the mouthpiece. "Porridge."

"*Porridge?*" The presenter laughed. "Funny choice for an evening meal isn't it?"

There was a loud crash. A figure burst out of the back door of the pub, one of the rugby players who'd been drinking in the public bar all afternoon. He began vomiting noisily against the low wall beside us.

"What's that?" The presenter's interest was suddenly peaked. "Sounds like someone being sick."

Steve smirked. "Yes, it's err… Jason. Doesn't quite have his sea legs yet."

"Or maybe your porridge wasn't to his liking Steve, eh? Ha!"

Smart-arse, I thought.

"Finally lads, is there anything from land you're missing already?"

I jerked my thumb towards the pub and tapped my watch. Last orders were in five minutes.

"A couple of beers in a nice warm pub would be nice," replied Steve, trying to keep a straight face.

"Yes, I'm sure. Ha! Ha! You'll have to work a bit harder for that now won't you boys, eh? Maybe in a couple more days once you hit land again. Ha! Ha!"

More like about five seconds once we get off the phone you fathead…

OUR PLANNED DEPARTURE date of May 1 came and went. Every day we postponed for lack of sponsorship was one less day to bike to Vladivostok in easternmost Russia, and launch *Moksha* before the Northern Hemisphere winter set in. Not thrilled about the prospect of freezing to death in Siberia, we decided to fix a cut-off date. If a title sponsor hadn't stepped up to the plate by June 1, we would either postpone until the following spring, or abandon the effort entirely. While the latter seemed almost unthinkable after the thousands of man-hours already invested, the former posed an equally dismal prospect: another soul-destroying year surviving on social security handouts and living in derelict housing.

They were desperate times, and desperate times can lead to reckless measures. *Moksha* still needed to be furnished with hundreds of bits of incidental gear—cups, plates, cutlery, saucepans, a kettle, food storage containers, batteries, a poo bucket for inclement weather, sponges for bailing, a handheld foghorn, fishing line, hooks—all of which cost money we didn't have. Taking matters into my own hands, I tried legging it from an East London marine supplier clutching a rubber bucket, two sponges, and a scrubbing brush. I got about twenty yards before being rugby tackled by a security guard outside Woolworths, bucket and sponges bouncing into the road, and a pair of old biddies looking on in disgust.

I was arrested and hauled off to Plaistow Police Station to be formally charged. I'd hit rock bottom, and braced myself for the worst. But after a stint in a holding cell, the booking officer became so intrigued by how a two pound fifty bucket to crap in was integral to the success of a human-powered circumnavigation of the planet, he let me go with a caution. My real punishment was yet to come, being read the riot act by Steve, justifiably livid at the integrity of the project so nearly compromised.

Sensing the whole thing was about to die on its feet, our families, and Steve's girlfriend, Maria, came to the rescue. The loan, repayable when sponsorship eventually materialized, was enough to pay off Hugo, finish *Moksha's* construction, and at least get us on our way. In many ways they had every reason not to. At the London Boat Show in January, when *Moksha* was brought in as a special feature by the show's organizer, numerous whiskery old sailing buffs had walked away shaking their heads after examining *Moksha*. One even declared the circumnavigation attempt to be one of the most sure-fire ways of committing suicide he'd ever seen.

Even then, we still didn't have near enough money for the entire trip. Faced with running out of funds in Eastern Europe, we changed the circumnavigation to a west-about route: biking south through France, Spain, and Portugal, before launching *Moksha* off the Algarve Coast and crossing the Atlantic to North America. Being a relatively young nation where the pioneering spirit was still celebrated, the US would hopefully offer a broader bite at the sponsorship apple. Properly financed, we could then pedal across the Pacific to Australia, aiming for a sister point to one already reached on the Atlantic. By hitting at least one pair of antipodes, defined as two points diametrically opposite each other on the Earth's surface, the expedition would meet the criteria for true circumnavigation laid out in 1971 by Norris McWhirter, founding editor of Guinness Book of Records: crossing all lines of longitude, the equator at least twice, and covering a minimum distance of 21,600 nautical miles, a distance equivalent to the circumference of the equator, thereby coming as close as possible to the geographic ideal of a great circle.

The route change produced another casualty, however. Still broke, having to sell his power tools to buy food, and dossing on the floor of an old water tower in Putney, Chris's continuing incentive to work on *Moksha* hinged around his promised role as support team driver. The revised route meant smooth roads as far as San Francisco. A full-on support team was no longer needed.

Another acrimonious falling-out ensued. Feeling he'd been used, Chris blew his top and stormed off the project. Steve took the news badly, angry that Chris should "abandon ship" before *Moksha* was fully finished. Although completed to design specifications, myriad small tasks still needed doing: painting, drilling holes for radio antennas, installing solar panels, sewing canvas compartment covers, fabricating a bed for the sleeping compartment, and so on.

I felt caught in the middle. In the overall interests of the expedition, my loyalty to Steve remained firm. Privately, however, as with Hugo, I didn't always agree with his methods, especially when it came to handling people whose goodwill and continued patronage we so relied upon, broke as we were. Those who fell by the wayside, claiming they'd been burnt, left a distinctly bad taste in the mouth.

Then again, Steve's single-mindedness and determination were what got the whole thing off the ground in the first place.

A DEPARTURE DATE of July 12 was set in stone. Kenny still didn't have his own camera, though. Repeated requests to the BBC and other UK broadcasters for even a loaner had drawn a blank, and we certainly couldn't afford one. What was the use in having a cinematographer along if he didn't have a camera? Out of options, Fingers from the squat staged an insurance job: renting a camera from a hire centre in Milton Keynes, having one of his cronies slip off the train with it en route back to Euston, then reporting it stolen.

The Guildford Street Gang threw a squat party to raise money for the cost of transporting *Moksha* to Portugal. Martin had volunteered to drive a van loaned by the international courier company DHL, towing a trailer borrowed from the metropolitan police Heavy Boats Section—the upshot of a serendipitous referral from the now friendly booking sergeant at Plaistow Police Station.

Plates of homemade vegetarian curry and rice were priced at four pounds, and wholesale beer and wine flogged at retail prices. Kenny rigged up a bungee jump in the back garden—a pound a pop—using shock cord cannibalized from an abdominal muscle builder, and bedsheets tied together. A couple of old mattresses tossed underneath offered a cursory nod to health and safety.

Aside from Catriona's friend breaking his arm, the night was a raging success. Nearly two hundred people turned up and cut loose. By the end of the night we'd raised over £1,500.

After just an hour of sleep, I tottered down to the kitchen to grab some breakfast. I had a meeting with a journalist from *Lonely Planet* at the Royal Geographic Society in half an hour.

The kitchen was a bombsite from the night before. Beer cans, wine bottles, and plastic cups filled with stale beer and cigarette butts strewn everywhere. The cupboards were empty of food. My eyes came to rest instead on a plastic container with the words SHIPS BISCUITS printed in black marker. Terry, a partygoer from Manchester, had taken the trouble to bake us some brownies for the Atlantic crossing.

What a nice guy, I thought, stuffing one in my mouth, another in my pocket. *No one will notice a couple missing, surely...*

I stepped over a pair of snoring bodies, grabbed one of the newly sponsored Madison Ridgeback mountain bikes, and tiptoed out the front door, closing it gently behind me.

Outside, it was a gloriously sunny July morning, and being a Sunday, the streets were virtually empty. Riding down Oxford Street I felt buoyant, euphoric even. I rode straight through a red light at Oxford Circus, swerving easily through traffic that seemed to move in slow motion. By the time I reached Marble Arch, my bicycle felt like a winged horse soaring above the clouds, the streets of London tapering to an elaborate tapestry of intricately woven threads below.

Bloody hell! Those Ships Biscuits are good shit!

I never made it to the interview. Somewhere between Marble Arch and Queensway I became distracted, dismounted Pegasus, and struck off into the wilderness of Hyde Park. Everything had become exuberant and scintillating, the viridescent leaves radiating a surreal, incandescent glow as they danced in the sunlight. Overhead the clouds had turned into freshly baked meringues. I was a panther now, crawling through the undergrowth, stalking lovers entwined on park benches, scaring the crap out of them as I leapt up from behind.

In the back of my mind, a voice was nagging: *You're leaving in less than 48 hours you dickhead, and there're still a gazillion things to do…*

The call to reason was lost, however, drowned by the roaring wind and crashing waves. A passer-by could have been forgiven for thinking they'd seen a drunk swaying in the branches of an elm tree that morning. What they really saw was a buccaneer swinging in the rigging of a brig somewhere off the Spanish Main, cutlass between his teeth, wrestling desperately with a topsail as the deck plunged in the swell.

EUROPE: *ON THE ROAD*

A journey can be either your death or your transformation.
—PAUL THEROUX, *The Happy Isles of Oceania*

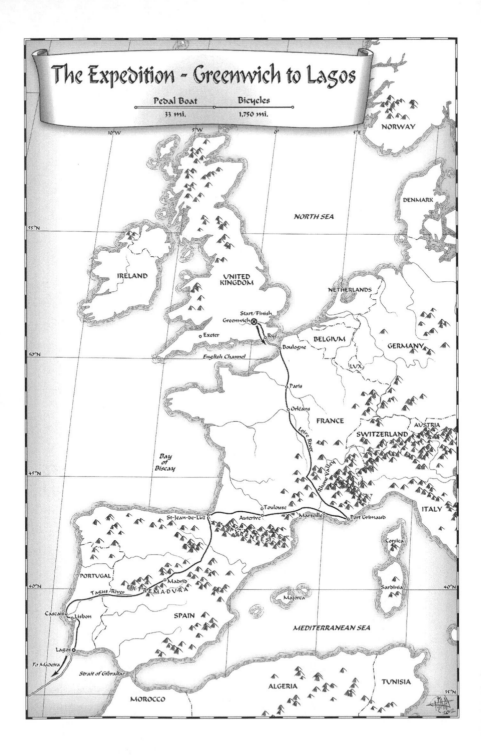

WHITE EXPEDITION TEE SHIRTS fluttering in the breeze, Steve and I stood straddling our bicycles, front tyres resting on a two-inch strip of brass embedded in the ancient cobblestones. Above us, fixed atop a spike like a giant cocktail cherry, a large crimson ball would drop at precisely 13:00 hours, as it first had in 1883 for ships on the River Thames to set their chronometers by. Our great journey was about to begin.

My heart drummed faster and faster as the seconds counted down. It was a tremendous moment, made even more so by the history surrounding us.

As the centre of all time and space, calibrating every clock and watch on the planet, the prime meridian of longitude held the keys to the nation's maritime past, and to our own futures. It was central to Britain establishing her superiority over the world's oceans at the peak of Empire. And, after travelling three hundred and sixty lines of longitude westwards, using the same navigational increments of degrees, minutes, and seconds that once steered our explorer ancestors to the farthest flung corners of the globe and back, we could also hope to return to the same point from which we started.

The noonday sun shone at its zenith above assembled family and friends. My sisters, Julia and Vicky, stood smiling supportively, holding the hands of my nephews Edward, George, and Freddie, still too young to really understand what their deranged uncle was up to now. Earlier, dear Vicky had pressed two Cadbury's chocolate bars into my hand. "For extra energy," she'd whispered encouragingly.

It would be a long time before I saw any of them again. Just how long, I had no way of knowing…

The world would have moved on unimaginably in thirteen years. My old Motorola "brick" cellular phone, so heavy I had to keep it in a bucket hooked to one end of a broom handle at the top of my window cleaning ladder, counter-balanced with half a bucket of water at the other end, would transform into a device no bigger than a credit card.

The Internet and climate change would be regular street talk, not just whispered conspiracy amongst geeks and tree huggers. Tony Blair would have come and gone. The franc, lira, and peseta replaced by the euro. Osama bin Laden and reality TV stars would be household names.

I glanced at Steve. His knuckles were chalk white from throttling the handlebars of his bike. His face was drawn with exhaustion. None of us had slept the past two days. At five am that morning, Kenny, Martin, and I were still vacating the squat, literally shovelling clothes and equipment into black rubbish sacks and tossing them into the back of the DHL van. I'd then pedalled hell for leather across London for a seven am interview at the *Sky News* studios in Isleworth, before backtracking via Hammersmith to close my account with Barclays. I'd walked out with £319.20 in my pocket, the sum total of my savings to circumnavigate the world.

"It should have dropped by now," Steve said, looking over his shoulder at the crimson ball. I checked my watch. It was four minutes past the hour. Was it stuck? Of all the days for Grandfather Time's one remaining ball not to drop...

"Sod it," I muttered. "Let's get on with it."

We grasped each other's forearms, nodded, and leaned into the first of some half billion pedal rotations. Waving to the cheering crowd, we swept out of the courtyard and entered an avenue of graceful sweet chestnuts, their verdant limbs bowing overhead in farewell bidding.

"A21," I HOLLERED ON our third lap of the roundabout, looking for the road south. "Where the fuck's the A21?"

Fifteen minutes into our multi-year journey, subsumed by the suburban wastes of South London, we were lost. We carried with us maps of France, the Pyrenees, the Algarve Coast, and navigational charts of the Atlantic, the Caribbean, and the North Pacific. We even had a star chart for celestial navigation. But where the hell was a London A to Z roadmap when you needed it?

Martin had already gone ahead in the van, *Moksha* in tow, to the coastal port town of Rye. It was from here that we would pedal across the Channel to Boulogne the next morning. As we dithered round the roundabout for the umpteenth time, Kenny appeared out of nowhere, riding pillion on a motorcycle driven by Paul from the Guildford Street Gang. They took the lead.

In a clear section of road ahead, the motorcycle slowed and drew alongside.

"Hoos it goon Steve?" shouted Kenny, camera levelled on his shoulder.

Steve was grinning ecstatically, happier than I'd ever seen him. "Fantastic! Three years of preparation, and we're finally on our way."

"Where to?"

"Francia, España, Portugal… *Woahh!*" He swerved suddenly to miss a bollard in the road. "And then, the Atlantic!"

We were the three musketeers riding side by side, *all for one, one for all*, wheels thrumming on the warm tarmac. I felt a surge of pride for my old college pal. We'd all worked hard to get to this point, but Steve had toiled the hardest and the longest, tirelessly coaxing his brainchild to life, mentoring it through a tricky adolescence to take on the world at last. If this was anyone's day, it was his.

The Kodak moment wasn't to last.

"Get aaht the fakin' road willya!" shrieked a bald, purple-faced man from the window of a Mini Metro. He swerved around us, engine revving wildly.

God, I can't wait to get away from Small Dick Syndrome, I thought.

Up ahead, Angry-Man-With-Small-Penis had pulled over. Incensed at having to slow down and go around us, he flung the driver's door open at the last second to catch one of us broadside. We veered around it easily. "What's your fuckin' problem?" Paul yelled, giving him the finger as we passed.

Two hours later, I discovered a use for second gear puffing up a hill near Sevenoaks. The confusion of London had slipped behind us at last, and untrammelled views of the South Downs rolled out in all directions. We splashed through pockets of deliciously cool air sweetened with the aroma of freshly picked strawberries. And turning left at Flimwell, a row of Oast Houses appeared. Decades had passed since any of them had been used to dry hops for beer—they'd all been converted into holiday homes. Nevertheless, they reminded me of a slice of England I would surely miss: lounging in a pub garden on a summer afternoon, gazing at the green rolling hills peppered with puff pastry sheep, getting quietly sozzled on Flowers IPA.

A wave of regret swept through me. I was at that Rubicon moment in any peregrination from the familiar. For only now, looking back over my shoulder, could I appreciate fully all I had ever known.

Crossing the Channel

I AWOKE IN darkness, disoriented, seagulls screeching overhead, salt smarting in my nostrils. This wasn't the squat. I lay there in my Buffalo sleeping bag, blinking at the shadows, letting the smell of the sea remind me where I was and what was I supposed to be doing.

Ah yes, of course. Circumnavigating the world by human power...

Something was buffeting and grinding against the stone quay beside me. *Moksha*, yawing at her mooring lines in the languid slop of the harbour, anxious to get going. Within the hour, Steve and I would be pedalling across one of the busiest waterways in the world, with its powerful tides and inshore currents, variable winds and innumerable obstacles.

Even if successful, we could look forward to being arrested on the other side, according to the French Coast Guard. Operating "unorthodox craft"—anything without a motor or a sail—was strictly illegal inside French territorial waters. The ruling made sense to prevent nitwits from paddling bathtubs or air mattresses into the paths of hundred-thousand-tonne super tankers. But for us, with a fully registered ocean-going vessel and support craft as accompaniment, it was ridiculous.

A fearful row had erupted over the whole affair leading up to our departure. The Dover Coast Guard appeared on national television, accusing Steve and I of foolhardiness for potentially costing the British taxpayer thousands of pounds and endangering the lives of those sent out to rescue us. Our response was to point out that if a monopoly over the Channel had always been surrendered to international shipping, we would all be speaking Spanish by now, the Armada having swept through in 1588 and invaded Britain unchallenged.

Unsurprisingly, our appeal to patriotic idiosyncrasy was ignored, and permission to leave from Dover summarily refused. Sneaking out from the less trafficked Rye nearly doubled the distance, dramatically increasing the odds against us with all the variables at play. But if we were intercepted leaving Dover, the expedition would effectively be over before it had even begun.

Half an hour later, the eastern sky tinged a lighter shade of blackened steel and a small crowd assembled on the wharf for last farewells. My parents stood stiffly to seaward, hair whipping in the breeze, expressions faithfully masking a cornucopia of suppressed fears and confusion as to why their only son was about to disappear over the horizon in something little bigger than a broom cupboard. My mother managed to hold it together until we embraced. Then her eyes welled.

Sensing I was about to lose it myself, I turned to the ladder leading down to *Moksha*. "Better get going," I sniffed.

HARBOUR BREAKWATER SAFELY astern, I aimed *Moksha's* nose at the French coast and flung myself at the pedals. The chain turned with a sharp urgency—*zzzzrrr… zzzzrrr… zzzzrrr*—the bow slicing through the calm water. Aside from a dull morning haze, the conditions were near perfect.

I turned to Steve. "How did your mum do with the farewells? Distraught?"

"No, stiff upper lip. I think she'd been to see one of her clairvoyants and found out I'm going to be okay."

"Did she tell you that?"

"No. But I figured she had, otherwise she'd be a lot more worried!"

I smiled. "Pass us a beer would you."

He fished for one of the cans of Castle Eden Ale rolling around the bottom of the boat. They were the only supplies we had apart from a sodden roll of toilet paper.

"We need a beer rack in here," said Steve, lobbing a can.

"And a loo roll holder." My body temperature had skyrocketed and sweat lashed across my face like driven rain. "I can't imagine this mode of transport will top my list for any future endeavours," I added in disgust.

Steve smirked. "Why doesn't that surprise me looking at you now?"

"Right. It's five thirty. I don't think I've ever had sweat coming off me this early. Have you? I feel like a sponge being squeezed of water."

"Beer, you mean."

"Maybe. But those carbohydrates are useful you know. The more I drink, the more I want to pedal."

"Piddle?"

"That too."

It was all silly gags in the euphoria of getting going, the grace period before some semblance of seriousness inevitably set in.

After two hours, it was time to change. "Okay you lazy sod," I said.

"Fancy doing some work?"

"Just let me have a quick fag first," Steve responded, reaching for a packet of cigarettes in the netting beside him.

Once on the pedals, it didn't take long for Steve's eyes to start bulging and his face reddening to the complexion of a beetroot. Too busy in London to get fit, we'd opted for an unorthodox exercise regime, one that involved waiting until it was time to go before starting to train. "Wait Training," Steve called it.

By nine thirty, we'd reached the edge of the Traffic Separation Scheme. Four enormous ships laden with containers emerged over the southwest horizon, migrating up the Channel like a plodding herd of brontosauruses. Except that motoring along at thirty knots they weren't plodding at all. With *Moksha's* top speed only a tenth of that, a fast walking pace at best, we were the lone pin on a bowling alley, four balls coming straight at us.

The voice of Bob Button, skipper of the *Snodgrass*, sprang to life on the radio. Thank goodness for the support boat!

"*Moksha*, there's a whole batch of ships coming up from the southwest. You've probably already seen them. We don't anticipate any problems. At the speed they're going, they'll be past us by the time we get there."

Nine hours later...

FRENCH VOICES ON the radio alerted us to the proximity of the forbidden shore, which remained indistinguishable from a low-lying cloudbank. As dusk fell, the sodium lights of Boulogne sputtered to life like tiny stars twinkling in the gloom, giving us something to aim for until the green and red channel marker buoys took us in the last half mile.

Where were the French authorities? Later, we found out it was Bastille Day, celebrated as a national holiday in France. Any Frenchman worth his salt was at home with his family, commemorating release from medieval feudalism with a special meal. We'd lucked out. For one day a year, the centuries-old rivalry with English *Rosbifs* was suspended.

Stuart, who had ridden across on the *Snodgrass*, was there to greet us on the wharf, ready and armed with a bottle of champagne. Shaking it vigorously, he proceeded to hose us down like a pair of Formula 1 drivers.

Celebrations were certainly in order. The expedition had reached its first foreign shore.

WE HIGHTAILED IT from Boulogne the next morning, before the French hangovers wore off and the harbour police twigged the appearance of a strange new craft in their marina. A hundred-franc note slipped into the pocket of the municipal crane operator had *Moksha* plucked from the water, and popped back on her trailer for the 1,600-mile overland journey to the Algarve Coast.

Steve and I would cycle the same distance—the length of France, over the Pyrenees to Spain, then hang a right into Portugal—keeping within a day's ride of the van to allow Kenny to film. *Moksha* would also be deployed for a series of planned media events in Paris, Madrid, and Lisbon, continuing our search for a title sponsor.

The first day back in the saddle was a short one, ending a mere fifteen miles down the coast at Hardelot, the first of 873 schools the expedition would visit over the next thirteen years. It was a chance to start gathering footage for our world citizenship film. The programme had been inspired by the Council for Education in World Citizenship, the same London-based charity that had secured HRH The Duke of Gloucester as our UK patron. The plan was to interview youngsters along the way, asking what environmental problems they thought the world would face after the year 2000, and what steps should be taken to combat them. The completed film would then be translated into different languages, and distributed to schools affiliated with the United Nations Educational Scientific and Cultural Organization (UNESCO), to inspire the decision makers of tomorrow.

Some of the children were also invited to express their views on the expedition, and asked, "Would *you* like to do it?"

"Noop," replied a carrot-headed boy on a student exchange from Leeds. "It costs too much money, it takes too long, and there's too much planning. It takes it all aaht o' yer!"

This was the same nine-year-old who, when asked if he thought people were starting to take global warming seriously, pointed out that people only *pretended* to be concerned when all they were *really* interested in was making money. And that *talking* about protecting the environment and actually *doing* something about it were two completely different things.

ON THE EVENING of July 19, while Kenny and Martin pushed on to Paris, Steve and I camped in a small wood near Amiens. It had been a long day. Ninety-five miles. I'd spent most of it wrestling with the baffling arsenal of new equipment apparently required for long distance cycling: twenty-one gears distributed between umpteen sprockets and levers, computerized odometer, SPD pedals that were murder to clip in and out of. The worst of it, however, was the spandex shorts, obscenely tight-fitting contraptions with a lurid spray-on look, making my balls stick out like two eggs in a hanky. French farmers smirked openly as I passed, and a lorry driver parked in a lay-by even threw his sandwich at me in disgust.

Only later did Steve inform me I was wearing them back to front.

While Steve gathered firewood, I laid out the supplies Martin had bought earlier in the day. French stick. Camembert cheese. Tomatoes. Bottle of plonk to anesthetize aching muscles. We sank back against our sleeping bags and gazed into the crackling fire. After all the pre-departure fuss it felt wonderful to be out in the wilds at last, drifting off to the chirruping crickets and other night sounds.

Next morning we found ourselves slipping effortlessly along an exquisitely smooth road, Northern France unfurling before us as a quilted patchwork of brightly coloured squares: luminous green fields of cabbages, chocolate earth under plough, mile upon mile of butter-yellow sunflowers thronging the roadside, their plate-sized heads bobbing approvingly as we passed. Occasionally, I felt the pitter-patter of tiny diaphanous wings. Out of the blue cloudless sky a dark shroud would drift across the road, a shimmering mass of greenfly migrating between over-fertilized fields, coating our sweating arms and legs like fly strips, and encrusting our hair with fluttering crowns of emerald sequins.

Dull smudges of wooded hills loomed in the distance, but the fields next to the road were treeless, empty of birdsong. Apart from the hum of our wheels, an eerie quietness prevailed.

Seventy-eight years previously, the landscape looked very different: scarred, blistered, and pulverized out of all recognition by the 1916 Somme Offense, the first day of which the British alone suffered 57,470 casualties. In the spring of 1992, before committing to the expedition full-time, I'd volunteered for the Commonwealth War Graves Commission in nearby Albert. Seventy-five per cent of the graves in cemeteries like Thiepval were unknown, the bodies unidentifiable or never recovered. Weeding around the chalk-white headstones, death echoing in the silent shadows of the towering memorial bearing some 72,000 names, I'd looked for clues to my perennial puzzle: *Life. How to live it?*

I imagined how, in that briefest of moments going "over the top," death lying face down in the mud a few paces away, life would have been revealed in its most raw and vital form. And how the experience of being, and of what ultimately mattered—of what *really, really fucking mattered*—come hurtling into hard, sharp focus.

Henry David Thoreau once said, "Rather than love, than money, than fame, give me truth. I sat at a table where were rich food and wine in abundance, and obsequious attendance, but sincerity and truth were not, and I went away hungry…"*

I wanted to know this same truth, but after a month of volunteering, I was none the wiser. Could I hope to find it in the merciless quarters of the ocean wilderness, I wondered?

WITH A NAKED woman on the back of every bus in Paris, advertising everything from dildos to microchips, leaving the city was easy. All we had to do was follow the finest pair of tits heading vaguely south, and set our male minds to autopilot.

Scruffy suburbs soon gave way to wide-open fields filled with barley and wheat. The traffic was relentless, and the French drove like lunatics. On the outskirts of Orléans, lounging in the saddle of the Loire Valley, we arrived hot and flustered after a series of poor directions to the Intermarché. Steve guarded the bikes while I hurried inside to grab a few things. When I emerged, he was chatting to two Arab youths slouched over their mopeds. A third was on his knees, rifling through the rear pannier of my bike.

"Hey!" I shouted. "What the hell do you think you're doing?" Setting down the bags of provisions, I marched towards him, stabbing my finger. "Get the *fuck* out of my pannier!"

Glaring at me in defiance, the thief stood and kicked my bicycle over. I returned the compliment, booting over his Lambretta 125cc hairdryer.

---

* *Walden* by Henry David Thoreau.

Then we were at each other's throats, tumbling across the tarmac in front of the supermarket entrance. My opponent fought dirty: biting, scratching, and pulling my hair. I retaliated with a highly sophisticated manoeuvre perfected in my *Goju-Ryu* karate days. "Knee in Bollocks."

Reaching to rip out one of his earrings, I caught sight of Steve. He was glancing anxiously between the other two youths, who looked equally paralyzed by indecision. Should they all launch in? Steve was clearly loath to do so. If we lost our bikes, we lost everything. Passports. Camping gear. What little money we had. End of expedition...

Two store detectives suddenly appeared, elbowing through the circle of gawking shoppers. My adversary promptly jumped to his feet, leapt onto the back of a speeding moped, and disappeared in a sputtering cloud of blue smoke.

Later, in the centre of Orléans, while I washed off the blood and grime in an ornamental fountain, Steve asked passers-by for directions to Vierzon. A bespectacled young man about to step into a car said he knew the way. He also happened to be an avid cyclist, spoke good English, and offered to put us up for the night in his nearby apartment.

While his girlfriend cooked a meal, Rimauld gave us some tips from his cycling adventures in different parts of the world.

"Zer experience of travelling depends on zer road you take," he said.

On the busier ones, he explained, we would see the same things in every country: screaming traffic, stultifying asphalt, miserable faces behind the wheel, and ugly roadside service stations selling over-priced, foul-tasting food. "But on zer leedle roads you can stop in zer villages, speak to real people, take in your surroundings wiz no distractions, experience zer real culture."

Much depended on the reason for setting out in the first place. "To win some kind of race looking at zer asphalt? Or learn somesing about zer world, maybe even yourself?"

As a practicing Buddhist, Rimauld talked in the same way about time. How it became compressed and all-powerful in the city, commanding subservience, but lost potency in the country, expanding and shedding its man-made skin, loosening its grip. Not until later in the trip would I understand what he was talking about. At the time—sinking into the velveteen couch, eyes drooping with fatigue, thinking longingly of my sleeping bag—he and his girlfriend were just two guardian angels who appeared uncannily in times of need, taking us in like strays, putting hot food in our bellies, before sending us on our way again, strength and spirit revitalized.

⚯

AT GIEN, HAVING followed the serpentine towpath along the Loire River, past leafy vineyards and fishermen hunched over the languid water and yet more swathes of golden sunflowers, Steve and I agreed to travel separately for a few days. The Atlantic crossing was fast approaching and playing on both our minds, making us increasingly edgy, withdrawn, and preoccupied with the reality of an undertaking only now starting to take shape.

Death would likely come in one of three forms: being washed overboard, collision with another ship, or running onto rocks or a coral reef. This was assuming the boat—Chris and Hugo's first since leaving boat building school—could handle big waves. I needed to spend a few days alone reconciling myself with the very real possibility of drowning at sea.

Steve would take the direct route over the Collines du Sancerrois and meet Kenny and Martin at a summer school in Brive. I would continue hugging the wide bend of the Loire valley to Orange, then cut across to the French Riviera to visit some old friends, Oliver and Marja, who ran an exchange bureau in Port Grimaud. The 1,000-mile detour meant pedalling an average of 150 miles a day to keep on schedule. This was welcome. I needed to build fitness for the Atlantic.

I descended 2,000 metres from the mountains above St. Etienne and entered the Rhone Valley. Thick clusters of giant plums, apricots, peaches, and pears sagged from branches overhanging the road, low enough to grab as I passed. For the last two days to Port Grimaud, I ate for free and on the fly.

Upon seeing me, my French hosts visibly heaved. Filthy and putrefying, dead insects splattering my face, chest, and hair, I resembled *un gril de radiateur*, apparently. Scarcely had I time to clean up and catch my breath when the phone rang. It was Kenny, sounding irate. How was he supposed to make a documentary about '*two guys goon roond the wrrrld*' if they were a thousand miles apart?

"I'll see ye in Auterive," he said, "say, in thir'y-six 'oors?" And without allowing for a reply, let alone a more realistic timeframe to be discussed, he hung up. I looked at my map. Auterive was over four hundred miles away.

Resentment boiled as I set out immediately for Marseille, cursing the expedition, Kenny, and the documentary series. It was the same imposition of limitations, the foisting of form and structure that I'd always railed against. At the age of three, I'd taken off from our home on the South Dorset coast, and was found by my mother several hours later heading for a bright shiny excavator five miles up the road. Twenty-three years on, I was still the wilful toddler being reined in.

Strange things happen when you're on a bike for a long time. After twenty-four hours of non-stop riding, my hands had turned into claws grasping the handlebars, and the middle three fingers on both hands become numb. The only way to bring back feeling was to shake them vigorously above my head, eliciting cheery waves from passers-by.

At six o'clock on the morning of August 1, calf muscles twitching with fatigue and my backside chafed raw, I collapsed on a bench in the town square of Auterive. Kenny rode up a short while later and tossed me a withered-looking croissant. When I proceeded to inform him that he was a "miserable slave-driving Scottish bastard," he just shrugged. "Tell me something ah don't knoo," he replied, and without further ado, began setting up his camera for an interview.

This was typical Kenny: no-nonsense, pragmatic, and acerbic. Most of the time, I cherished him for it—they were invaluable qualities to have in an expedition teammate. Today, however, his indifference only galled me further.

Three days later, having regrouped on the Atlantic coast at Saint-Jean-de-Luz, Steve and I began the long haul over the Pyrenees. After fourteen miles and a 3,000-foot rise in elevation, taking in steepening grades, narrowing switchbacks, and diminishing oxygen, we would reach the Spanish Navarra Plateau.

We'd been on the road only three weeks, but already I'd discovered that tackling mountains on a bicycle boiled down to two things: extreme pleasure, and extreme pain, with only the rider, the bike, and a little willpower separating the two. The worst thing you can do on a long climb is to stop, getting going again being hellish. Still, the temptation to get off and lie down by the side of the road got stronger the higher up we went. Aches and pains started popping up in places I never knew even existed. It was at times like these, I concluded bitterly, that the bicycle was little more than a barbaric tool invented by some sick, sadistic bastard bent solely on inflicting misery and suffering on others.

Darkness fell. It began to rain. We kept climbing, becoming engulfed by thickening layers of mucilaginous mist—a real pea souper. Heavily laden trucks groaned past in low gear, headlights picking out tendrils of ghoulish vapour curling up from the glistening tarmac, hissing tyres throwing up all manner of filth into our faces. For many, this would have been a nightmare. For Steve and I, it was what the expedition was all about: getting closer to the edge, that fine line between comfort and calamity, where life and the experience of living it starts to get more vivid and more interesting.

A storm was sweeping up the valley from the north. Thunder boomed all around, and lightning flashes threw freakish shadows against the sheer rock wall carved out for the mountain pass. With every strike, an imprint of the surrounding trees blanched freeze-frame into my retinas. Then, another hairpin, and we emerged from the ceiling of cloud into a crystal clear night blazing with stars.

Steve stopped at the summit, admiring the light show in the valley below.

"Incredible isn't it!" he marvelled as I drew up alongside.

All I could do was nod, my breath coming in shallow rasps.

We were now looking down onto the storm. Molten rivers of electricity streaked through the cloud tops from one side of the valley to the other. It was mesmerizing, hypnotizing, and utterly magnificent.

But after a few minutes, we were both shivering. The heat generated from the climb had evaporated into the night, leaving a sodden chill seeping in around the edges of our mortal coils, sapping the moment.

We shared a packet of biscuits and a Mars Bar, pulled on our fleeces, and started the long descent to Pamplona.

"DID YE SEE any livestock in this field?" Kenny asked, lifting his bike over what seemed an unusually high fence.

I pushed my panniers through the lower strands and joined him on the other side. "Nope. Just those two dozy-looking things back there by the side of the road."

"They had horns oan them, right?"

"Of course, they're cows."

"I mean big bastard horns."

"Dunno. Didn't see properly."

We walked our bikes over to where Steve was already setting up camp in a stand of cork trees. For once, there were no thorns, no biting ants, and no yapping dogs. The sweet aroma of cork pervaded the air, and the last rays of the sun collapsed into a milky haze rolling in from the west. Apart from the bedtime chatter of birds in the branches above us, the air was silent.

Carving out large chunks of the map, we'd blazed a trail from the Pyrenees twelve days previously, riding hundred-plus mile days across fabulously sun-bleached landscapes steeped the colour of pale straw to Madrid. West of the capital, the country became even harsher, evident by the weather-beaten expressions of the old-timers who scowled as we passed, skin wrinkled and folded like the surrounding hills of the Extremadura. We were now just a half hour's ride from crossing the Spanish-Portuguese border.

Earlier, whilst rummaging in my panniers for loose pesos to change into escudos, I discovered I'd left my passport back in England. I hadn't needed it until now. We'd sneaked into Boulogne unannounced and swept into Spain unchallenged, the guard fast asleep at the checkpoint on the Autopista del Cantabrico. Portugal, however, being a relative newcomer to the European Economic Community, would be a different story.

Steve threw a fit. I had two favourite tricks, apparently. Not listening to any instructions. Then denying all knowledge once I'd forgotten them. We were on a tight schedule, he pointed out. The time it took for the passport to be tracked down at my parent's house in Dorset and sent to the nearest town might mean missing our weather window to depart on the Atlantic.

Just as Steve found my cavalier attitude irksome, his leadership style set my teeth on edge. Even with the week apart, tension between us had been steadily building. In the good old days, we could have sat down over a beer, laid our respective baggage out in the open, and laughed about it afterwards. The pressures of being on an expedition had frayed the edges of our friendship, however. The former transparency had been replaced by laboured tolerance. And the unfortunate catch-22 of diminishing dialogue is the corresponding difficulty in resolving disputes that require dialogue.

Like dutiful Brits, we resorted to a silent standoff instead.

In truth, the real cause of our discontent ran deeper than either of us realized. Robert Louis Stevenson once noted that, "Every durable bond between humans is founded in, or heightened by, some element of competition." An unspoken rivalry had always existed between Steve and I, taking root in the seedbed of student hijinks, each trying to upstage the other in our wild escapades. Out on the road, competitiveness still lurked, only the stakes were now much higher. The expedition involved several years of commitment, a mound of debt to be repaid, and the real possibility of one or both of us getting seriously injured or even killed. What had once been little more than two friends clowning around for kicks was now a much more serious affair.

I AWOKE NEXT morning to heavy breathing. Opening my eyes, I saw an enormous black bull just a few feet away, nuzzling one of my rear panniers, the one containing our toasties and apricot jam. Its horns were, indeed, big bastard horns: five feet across with an impressive domed boss in the middle. Great snorting puffs were billowing from the animal's nostrils.

I closed my eyes. *That's why the fence was so high getting in here last night...*

When I opened them again, the bull had moved. It was standing over Steve's red sleeping bag, bringing to mind a disturbing scene I'd watched on television in a bar in Madrid: a matador, tangled on the ground in his red *muleta*, being repeatedly skewered by a similar-looking brute.

Careful not to draw attention to myself, I slowly zipped up my sleeping bag and lay perfectly still. I didn't have the heart to warn Steve. In fact, a part of me secretly hoped he'd get the shish kebab treatment too after being such a shit over the passport affair.

"Bastard!" he cried when I recounted the incident over breakfast, "Why didn't you warn me?"

"Didn't want to piss it off," I replied, implying that I had his best interests at heart all along. "Your sleeping bag had it riled up enough as it was."

Kenny looked up from the viewfinder of his camera. "If somethin' like that happens again," he said enthusiastically, "let me know so I can switch ma camera oan fust, okay? It's awl been a bit tame so far. Someone gettin' hurt would be great fur th' documentary."

A little later, Kenny rode ahead as we approached the border. The only evidence of there actually being one was a small wooden hut in the middle of the road. A shake of his head would mean police, at which point I would pull off the road and try to sneak around through the trees. Drawing level with the checkpoint, he gave a couple of nods instead. The border was unmanned. Lady Luck had smiled on me once again.

AFTER SNAKING DOWN the spectacular Tejo Valley, bisecting towns like Alviga where old men sat in backyards watching their fruit grow—the pace of life so laid back it was uncertain as to whether there even was a pace—and every male under the age of thirty was *futebol louco* and spent his life in a roadside bar yelling at a television set, we rolled into Lisbon.

We spent a week at the accommodating Clube Naval de Cascais, painting *Moksha* a final coat of white, and pumping club members for knowledge of the Algarve coast. Originally, the plan was to leave from the fishing hamlet of Sagres perched on the southwesternmost tip of the continent, to get us away from the rocky coast and into the Atlantic as quickly as possible. But after consulting Charles Lindley, the club secretary, the larger seaside resort of Lagos fifteen miles to the east was proposed. An acquaintance ran the newly built marina there. A quick phone call landed us a complimentary base of operations to prepare for the big crossing, complete with a crane to launch *Moksha*.

The only problem was getting there. A suspension bridge spanning the Tagus River conveniently connected Lisbon to the south of the country, but only motorized vehicles were allowed to use it. What to do? Using human power every step of the way was one of the fundamental tenets of the circumnavigation.

"Let's just swim the river," I suggested. "It's only a mile across. Martin can take the bikes across in the van."

"Aye, so long as you dinnae swallow any o' it," Kenny replied. "There's a ruddy great nuclear power station upstream."

And that was how, on the morning of August 29, Steve and I found ourselves pedalling like the clappers in the slowest lane of the three-lane expressway leading over the outlawed bridge. The towering superstructure loomed rust red in the morning sunshine, much like its illustrious sister in San Francisco, the Golden Gate Bridge. A sign appeared that needed no translation: *"Proibido!"* with symbols for a cyclist, pedestrian, and horse-drawn cart posted underneath. According the Clube Naval's Luis Steves, our chances of success were slim. Even if we made it to the other side without being arrested, a line of tollbooths and police barriers would block our escape.

The gradient increased. The tarmac gave way to a gridiron frame, affording glimpses of the river flashing far below. Near the halfway point, we caught sight of a police motorcyclist parked in the nearside lane. He was leaning over the driver's side window of a family sedan, writing out a fine. His helmet jerked up as we passed. Seconds later, we were overtaken by a flurry of flashing lights and howling sirens.

Dismounting, the cop looked us up and down with utter contempt. We were both shirtless, our naked torsos streaked with sweat. Riding a bicycle across the revered April 25th Bridge—a national icon commemorating the end of fifty years of political tyranny—was obviously bad enough. Doing it half-naked was adding insult to injury, the equivalent of streaking through Westminster Abbey with your pecker hanging out.

The safest thing to do in the circumstances was for the policeman to escort us to the south side of the bridge, extract a fine, and send us on our way. But the south side was exactly where we wanted to go, something the cop knew only too well, of course, and he wasn't about to give us the satisfaction.

Opting instead for the infinitely more perilous—but for him rewarding—alternative, he marched out into the middle of the motorway with leather-gloved hand outstretched, and brought all three lanes of rush hour traffic to a screeching halt. Beckoning with his other hand, he then signalled for us to walk the walk of shame. A tirade of abuse from the waiting drivers followed. Some mouthed obscenities from behind their windscreens. Others leaned out of their windows and shook their fists. Reaching the median, the officer repeated the procedure: riding out in front of the northbound traffic, lights flashing, and shooing us across.

Satisfied the pestilent English had been suitably disgraced and Portuguese pride avenged, the cop shot us one last scornful look, and accelerated back towards Lisbon. We had no choice but to follow.

The frustration on Steve's face said it all. "We were so close!"

I watched the motorbike disappear from view. "Fuck this," I muttered, turning my bike around. "Let's go." I began pedalling back up the ramp towards the centre span, riding against the traffic.

With no hard shoulder, the only option was to weave between the vehicles, missing bumpers and wing mirrors by inches. *What a rush!* My heart was pounding. *Now we're really grabbing life by the balls!*

We were met with a near-universal impassioned response from the motorists, a cacophonic onslaught of blaring horns, lewd gestures, and howled obscenities:

"*Você é louco!*" You're crazy!

"*Saia da estrada de você maniacs fodendo.*" Get out of the road you fucking maniacs.

"*Hey você filhos do cadelas estúpidos! Você quer começ matado?*" Hey you stupid sons of bitches! You want to get yourselves killed?

"This is crazy!" Steve yelled behind me.

Cars were now coming at us head-on, literally trying to push us off the bridge. A man jumped out of his van to try to grab me. *What's wrong with these people?* I thought. It was hard to reconcile the sudden regard for road safety with the unswerving examples of recklessness we'd witnessed since entering the country.

The only option was to return to the other side.

Ducking under a pair of outstretched arms, I nipped behind a bus, dismounted to cross the central divide, and pushed off into the fast lane, heading south once again.

Okay, back in business...

I glanced over my shoulder. Steve was nowhere to be seen.

Shit, where is he?

The line of tollbooths appeared. One of the lounging police officers caught sight of me.

"*Parada! Parada!*" he shouted, waving his arms and striding purposefully into the road.

No going back now, I thought. Besides, I was shifting coming off the apex of the bridge; my bike computer read eighty-three kilometres per hour.

I swept unchallenged through an empty toll lane.

A minute later I heard a loud beeping, and turned to see a pasty-faced paramedic jabbing his fingers at me from the window of an ambulance. *"Pleece! Pleece!"* he was saying. "You have to *estop! Pleece* go back for *pleece…"*

I smiled and picked up the pace. What was he going to do if I didn't *estop?* Run me over? At least he could then take me to hospital…

THE AMBULANCE GAVE up the chase a mile later. I hid behind a grassy mound to watch for Steve. But after half an hour, there was no sign. I began to fear the worst. *He's probably in a police cell by now,* I thought guiltily.

Just then, he appeared, looking euphoric.

"What happened?" I exclaimed. "Thought you'd been arrested!"

Steve was laughing and gasping for breath. "Nearly was. It was fucking insane back there, wasn't it? I crossed over to the other side like you did, but the cops were already waiting. Half a dozen of them ran over and clobbered me."

"And?"

"They tried to extort money. 'You pay money for fine'. You know, the usual bullshit."

"How much?"

"Seven thousand escudos—ridiculous. I told them I didn't have it. 'Okay,' they said, 'we take your passport, and you come back tomorrow with money'. I lied and told them I didn't have a passport, either."

"Then?"

"Eventually they got bored and let me go."

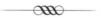

THE FIRST MORNING in Lagos, I awoke on the move. Scouting around for somewhere to sleep, I'd found an abandoned carriage in the railway yard. It turned out, however, that the dilapidated trains servicing

Portugal's rail network only looked incapable of going anywhere. Dragging my sleeping bag behind me, I bailed out onto the platform before the thing got up a head of steam and hauled me back to Lisbon.

Steve and I had rolled into town the afternoon before, taking a day to complete the 145 miles from the April 25th Bridge. Martin and Kenny had already unloaded the contents of the van into a storage room on loan from the marina. His duty complete, Martin started on the long journey back to London. He'd done us proud. As well as delivering *Moksha* safely, he'd given Steve and I a much needed crash course in bike maintenance, and taught us how to cook vegetarian food so that dull root crops like turnips and squash didn't taste like cardboard.

The next few weeks became a blur of activity squaring away thousands of last minute details. Steve concentrated on fitting *Moksha's* radar reflector and solar panels, and sewing the canvas bed and compartment covers in place. Kenny applied his knowledge of all things electrical to install the wiring system. I, meanwhile, focused on the food, medical kit, and safety equipment. As the days passed, my "to do list" grew longer rather than shorter. Divorced from the usual support systems taken for granted on land, the number of things needed for a human being to go to sea was truly staggering.

Worst-case scenarios had to be assumed for everything. We had antibiotics for bacterial infections. But what about a shark bite? Doctor's clinics were scoured for a suture kit to close open wounds. The Royal Air Force had donated a pair of lifejackets and one-person life rafts should *Moksha* sink. But what if the hull sustained only superficial damage from floating debris? A sheet of flexible PVC board was cut into sections to staple gun to the outside of the hull, slowing a leak enough to keep going.

Water was the biggest concern, space on *Moksha* being too limited to carry enough for the entire voyage. A handheld desalinator pump would convert seawater into fresh, an hour of pumping producing a little under one gallon. But what if it failed? A visit to the local hardware store supplied the materials to bodge together a freshwater still as emergency backup: boiling saltwater in a kettle, the steam condensing inside a length of copper tubing coiled inside a bucket of cold seawater.

To allay any fears my crewmate had of dying a slow, painful death from dehydration, I laid on a demonstration.

"We can present this to the Science Museum when we're finished," I said proudly, positioning a saucepan under the outlet pipe. Any moment, freshwater would start pouring out, I was certain.

Steve eyed the contraption with thinly veiled scepticism. The kettle had been boiling for several minutes and produced only billowing clouds of steam. "I doubt it," he replied. *"Playschool* perhaps."

Ten minutes later, a single drop appeared.

"Look at that!" I cried, pointing in triumph.

"Yeah, almost enough for a cup of tea right there…"

Next it was working out how best to stow everything. All the food and equipment first had to be weighed on a set of bathroom scales to make sure *Moksha* floated level in the water. Too front heavy, and her bow would spend most of its time buried in the back of the next wave, slowing us down. Too much weight in the stern, and she'd pull the marine equivalent of a wheelie, again producing too much drag. All of it then had to be lashed down with netting below the waterline. If we capsized and the stores ended up on the roof, *Moksha* would remain belly up and start sinking. Proper stowage was vital. It was the key to her self-righting mechanism.

Although tortuously cramped and blisteringly hot inside the unventilated fore and aft compartments, the final act of stowage made the long-anticipated voyage come alive. Like packing your suitcase before going on holiday, it felt like we were finally going somewhere. Except, in this case, the last thing it was going to be was a holiday…

Which was why, if we worked hard by day, we played even harder by night. As departure day approached, our nocturnal exploits were fuelled by the urgency of living each moment to the max, possibly our last on land if something went wrong on the voyage. Lagos being a den of iniquity didn't help. Already gaining a reputation as one of Southern Europe's hottest party destinations, there were plenty of honey pots to dip our sticky paws into. The last nail in the coffin of sobriety was Stuart arriving from London.

Renting an apartment in the centre of town, he quickly scoped out the liveliest bars, befriending a colourful array of characters in the process, including California Carlos, who, we decided, was either an arms dealer, or a drug runner, probably both. Every afternoon around the cocktail hour, Carlos would swing by the marina and "shoot the shit" in his Marlon Brando drawl.

"How's the old wazzoo today, Jason?" he asked one evening. His grin was more lopsided than usual, complementing the distinctive Roman nose.

Two nights before, I'd suffered an unfortunate mishap on my bicycle. It was all Stuart's doing. Earlier in the evening, he'd popped out of the apartment ostensibly in search of medicine for an upset stomach—consequence of the previous night's revelry. Two hours later, he was back with two gorgeous German girls instead. He'd met them in *Zanzibar*, he said, reeling them in with the by now time-honoured line: *"Come and meet the guys who are going to do it!"*

At two o'clock in the morning, I found myself riding at high speed through the cobbled streets, heading for the marina lockup where I knew there was a packet of condoms. Aside from a blanket wrapped around my shoulders, I was naked, fresh from the passionate embrace of my German sweetheart. Entering the town square, I took the corner a little too sharply. The blanket slipped and jammed in the front wheel, locking it dead, and launching me head first over the handlebars.

By the time I made it back to the apartment, bloodied and bruised, my *kleiner vogel*, my little bird, had flown. Just as well. I'd landed plum on my *wiener schnitzel*, rendering it inoperable with road rash.

AFTER WEEKS OF adverse winds howling from the south, forcing the departure date to be postponed repeatedly, a ridge of high pressure formed over the Azores, giving us our weather window to punch far enough from the coast before the winter storms set in.

Sitting in the marina toilet the eve of departure, I placed a video camera on the sink opposite, and prepared to record my first video diary. "Don't worry, it's arsehole proof," Kenny had said, handing me a list of questions. "Even ye can wuk it."

I pressed the red record button.

What do you think you and Steve will miss from land?

"Toilet paper for one thing." My voice echoed off the tiled interior. "For the next three months, it'll just be the power of the sea…"

On *Moksha*, defecating would involve hanging over the side and splashing our arses with seawater. A test-run using the bidet proved a complete disaster. The Continental European habit of squirting cold water up one's bottom was definitely going to take some getting used to.

I finished up and joined Steve outside on the dock. He was standing next to a yachtie, squinting at a bucket of water through a triangular-shaped contraption with dials, mirrors, coloured lenses, and a telescope. Less than a day before leaving, he was getting his first lesson in how to use a sextant.

THE ATLANTIC
INTO THE BIG BLUE

So one forgets oneself, forgets everything, seeing only the play of the boat with the sea, the play of the sea around the boat, leaving aside everything not essential to that game in the immediate present. One has to be careful though, not to go further than necessary to the depths of the game. And that is the hard part... not to go too far.

—Bernard Moitessier, *The Long Way*

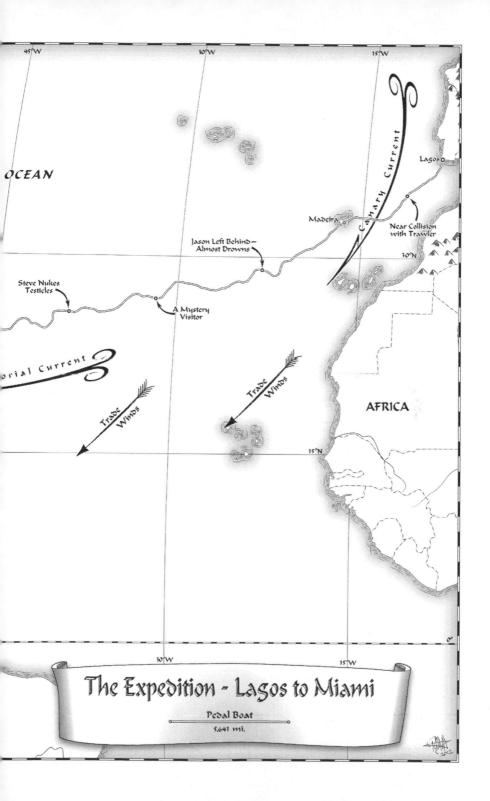

The Expedition - Lagos to Miami

Pedal Boat

5,641 mi.

A GAGGLE OF WELL-WISHERS had gathered at the dockside to see us off. They'd been waiting since dawn, our intended time of departure, but a last all-night bender, customary for sailors embarking on long ocean voyages from which they might never return, had us staggering down the gangplank three hours later than advertised.

"Crack ay noon as usual?" Kenny quipped, levelling his camera at Steve's washed-out face.

"Just keeping to nautical tradition," Steve mumbled in defence, trying not to sound as buggered as he looked.

The mood was sombre. Shortly after vacating Stuart's apartment, an entire bottle of Jägermeister, a complimentary gift from Zanzibar Jim, had slipped through my fingers and exploded on the floor of the lift. The sickly-smelling fluid seeped its way under our sandals on the way down to the ground floor, turning our already fragile stomachs.

Stuart looked horrified. "Hope you haven't jinxed the voyage, Jason!"

Steve and I climbed gingerly aboard *Moksha*, and prepared to cast off from the floating pontoon. Just then, Barry Sadler, a kindred sailing spirit and member of the local expatriate community, pushed a plastic container filled with dried figs and nuts into each of our hands.

"You're probably going to argue over food," he said with a knowing wink. "So I've labelled them accordingly." One read 'His', the other 'Mine'. *Seems a bit unnecessary*, I thought. *Won't we be sharing everything?*

It wasn't until a fortnight into the voyage, and our appetites were raging with the 8,000-plus calories consumed each day, that I understood how quickly human beings revert to their base animal selves when faced with diminishing resources.

I took the first shift, pedalling up the broad, flat channel leading from the harbour to the sea. As we rounded a red and white striped navigation beacon marking the southeastern corner of the breakwater,

a gentle swell picked up *Moksha's* bow, and she lunged forward in anticipation of the open Atlantic. God, it felt good to be leaving Lagos! The
wild partying had worn thin, and our health was beginning to suffer.
Stuart had a stomach ulcer, and I was having to inject myself in the
backside twice a day for a dose of the clap I'd picked up from a local
waitress. In the final days leading up to departure, while everyone else
was slaving away on boat preparations, I'd been sneaking off for a bit
of how's-yer-father in Stuart's apartment. Now I was paying full price
for truancy.

A prawn trawler laden with last night's catch chugged past, seagulls
wheeling and crying overhead. Another half mile and we passed the
honeycombed cliffs of the Sagres Peninsula, glowing rich golden brown
in the morning sunshine. A small red observation tower shaped like
a miniature lighthouse was the only interruption in an otherwise unbroken skyline. A lone figure, a tourist perhaps, was standing at the
pinnacle.

Five hundred years ago it might have been Henry the Navigator
standing atop this same vantage point, telescope outstretched, watching the tiny rectangles of swollen canvas shrink to faint specks before
finally disappearing under the western horizon. Capitalizing on recent
advancements in marine technology, improvements that had lead to
the development of square-rigged sailing ships sophisticated and spa-
cious enough to carry sufficient supplies and men for long haul ocean
crossings, Henry was one of the early driving forces behind the Golden
Age of Exploration. Both Vasco de Gama and Christopher Columbus
had passed this way in the latter half of the fifteenth century. And perhaps the most ambitious of them all, Ferdinand Magellan, struck out
from the coast in one of five ships bound for the East Indies in 1519.
Of a total crew list numbering 237, just eighteen men returned three
years later, exhausted, riddled with scurvy, and manning just one ship,
the *Victoria* (Magellan was killed on the remote island of Mactan in

present-day Philippines). The return of even one vessel was hailed as a triumph. Not only was the cargo of cloves and cinnamon worth a fortune, the voyage heralded one of the greatest feats in maritime history: the first circumnavigation of the globe.

Choosing such an auspicious point to depart from on our own debut voyage was no coincidence. The same prevailing clockwise pattern of winds and currents that aided Magellan's first leg to South America would put us on track to Miami. Throw a stick off the southeast coast of Portugal, and it'll wash up on a beach in the Caribbean eventually. Sailing, or in our case, pedalling, simply speeds things up.

Five hours into the voyage, the VHF radio crackled to life. It was Stuart, speaking from our support boat, *Petronella*, signalling they were ready to head back to Lagos. Kenny had all the footage he needed, and we were now safely past any danger of being washed onto the rocky headland of Cape St. Vincent, the last land before the Americas. It was time for us to get on with it alone.*

"You're coming up fine on the radar!" yelled Stuart, now standing less than thirty feet away as *Petronella* made a final pass. His words were reassuring. The last thing we needed on day one was to be mowed down by an oil tanker. All the old sailing farts in their stuffy club lounges back in England, the same ones who'd told us we wouldn't last a day in such a ridiculous contraption, would turn to each other, and boast, "I told the fools myself, but they wouldn't listen!"

Eight die-hard friends waved final farewells from the rail. I could make out the outline of California Carlos's snout. "Save your wind!" he called hoarsely as Steve returned a final *toot-a-toot-toot* on our handheld foghorn, a response to the lone baritone blast from *Petronella*. The sound of engines grew fainter, and Stuart's craggy features scowling over the

---

* Having a support craft all the way to Miami would have been not only prohibitively expensive, but a liability. A larger craft coming alongside *Moksha* in rough seas would potentially cause untold damage.

stern rail faded from view. Considering how much childish delight I'd seen in his eyes over the past few weeks, it was disconcerting to see the face of a concerned parent looking back. How must my family, in particular my mother, be feeling at this time? When I'd telephoned them the previous evening to bid final farewells, my father had asked whether I'd remembered to make a will. "For what?" I'd replied. "I don't own anything." It wasn't so much what to bequeath in material terms, he pointed out, as it was what I wanted done with any "bits that might come bobbing back." Burial or cremation?

Then we were on our own. A thick veil of silence descended all around, muffling our ears like a blanket. I closed my eyes. Only the sound of water lapping against the hull and the gentle undulation of the boat gave any clue as to where we were...

A mile from shore, with no support boat, reality was finally sinking in. For years it had all been theory, just *talk, talk, talk*. Now we actually had to go out and do the thing we'd been banging on about.

My eyes snapped open. "Steve, what the *fuck* have you got us into here mate?"

He laughed. "Not sure to be honest." He was grinning that goofy expression of his that meant, *'Don't ask me!'*

"So... what if we decide this is a really, really bad idea and wanted to, err—"

"Abort the voyage?" Steve raised his eyebrows. "Well, at this point, we can't."

"Rubbish. You're joking, right?"

He shook his head. "Take a look at the pilot charts. The Canary Current runs about a knot down the east coast of Portugal before turning west. I'd say we were in it already. We're going across the Atlantic whether we like it not."

I put my head in my hands, and thought, *Oh god, what have I done?*

October 14. Day 7. 250 miles south of Lagos

STEVE UNSCREWED THE cap off the syringe, took careful aim, and buried the needle into my right buttock using a little more force than seemed necessary.

"Ouch you bastard," I winced. "You didn't need to stick it in that hard!"

"Keep still," he hissed, pushing the plunger in all the way. "Anyway, it's your last dose. Perhaps driving the point home will teach you to be a little more careful in future."

Fair point. Pissing through razor blades four times a day for the next three months would have been excruciating.

"I vud heff no choice," he continued in an exaggerated Doctor Mengele voice, waggling a blunt fruit knife in the direction of my weeping member, "but to resort to major surgery, ent viz no anaesthetic!"

We were a week into the voyage, and starting to adapt to our strange new world of water. The first few days had been horrendous, any attempt to hold down food quickly followed by a violent episode of projectile vomiting into the drink. Even the *thought* of "Bacon and Beans," an ambitious attempt by the British Army to cram an entire greasy English breakfast into a single foil bag, was enough to send either of us lunging for the side. And on the third morning, we'd solved the riddle of why all the *Duncan's of Scotland* milk chocolate had gone mouldy. The army rations were six years out of date.

But now our stomachs had stabilized, and confidence in *Moksha* was growing daily. We were getting the hang of how she moved on the briny, twisting and turning with dolphin-like grace in response to each passing wave. It was like riding a mechanical bull: hips gyrating, upper bodies compensating to maintain balance. You needed a free hand ready to catch hold when making a cup of tea or taking a whiz over the side. Otherwise, a sudden incoming wave would fling you against the side of the cabin, sending scalding tea into your lap, or pee running down your legs.

After a few days of experimenting, we settled on two-hour pedal shifts during the day, and three at night. The person on break could slide his weary body feet first into the stark, no-frills sleeping compartment with dimensions comparable to a snug coffin. The Davy Jones Express—so named by the droll boat builders—hadn't always been so joyless. It had left the boatyard in Exeter with *Razzle Readers Wives* pages glued to the roof, an embellishment The Duke of Gloucester noted with hearty approval when inspecting *Moksha* before her River Thames launch.

Though claustrophobic at first, the Rathole (as it later became known) quickly became the most prized real estate on the boat, being the only place a person could stretch out fully and relax.

The only other place to rest was sitting opposite the pedaller on a rudimentary plywood box. Here, a plethora of tasks always needed doing: navigating, repairing equipment, cooking a meal on the little propane stove hanging beneath a cannibalized pannier rack, and so on.

A big incentive for having someone constantly on the pedals, eyes scanning the horizon 24/7, was the drastically reduced chance of colliding with another ship. With the horizon only eight miles away, our biggest fear was waking to the throb of diesel engines, and capsizing under a giant bow wave, then being rolled by thousands of tons of laden steel. Massive propellers would finish the job, pulverizing us into fish food. Apart from a skipped stroke in the engine's cadence, the crew would never know they'd hit anything.

Night-time brought its own special flavour to this strange dollhouse existence. Pedalling without a moon was like being immersed in a sensory deprivation tank—total blackout. Only the peristaltic rhythm of the sea gave a sense of kinaesthesia. Up. Down. Side to side. Now rolling. Now pitching. We'd run out of time to fit a compass light before leaving Lagos, so navigating in darkness meant lining up a lone star with the corner of the hatchway to keep on course. Every thirty minutes or so a different pinprick had to be chosen, to account for the Earth's rotation. Only the navigator's keystone, the North Star, remained stationary.

Otherwise, our minds were free to wander for hours through the winding corridors of childhood memories, future aspirations, and present concerns. We called this Mind Travelling, which, depending on how exhausted we were, ranged from focused and quite useful analysis of ideas, to the mind behaving like a demented Ping-Pong ball, bouncing from one train of trivial associations to the next, until the starting point was long forgotten.

It was while lost in thought in the early hours of the eighth morning that movement caught my eye: lights bobbing up and down behind the inky black crests of the waves, far off the port beam. *There it is again...* Leaning forward to see better through the open hatch, I could see that it was a ship all right. But how far away, and what direction was it heading?

Before leaving London, Steve and I had been put through a Yacht-master's course, free of charge, by a kindly instructor who must have twigged how clueless we were, and felt bound by conscience to impart enough knowledge to keep us alive for at least the first week. While Tony Isard's thorough, albeit textbook nautical education provided us with basic navigation skills and a rough understanding of the rights of way on the ocean highways, it was no substitute for the real thing.

The waves subsided long enough to make out a green and red light beneath a single white light. This meant a vessel heading towards us, rather than away. And with only one masthead light, it was under fifty metres. But what was the lower, even brighter light radiating into the night like a sodium floodlight? I cast back through the Lights and Shapes section of the course. Nothing sprang to mind.

What the hell is that thing?

Continuing to pedal, I kept track of the small procession of Christmas tree lights through the polycarbonate windows. The strange thing was they didn't seem to be altering course. With *Moksha* so low in the water, perhaps they couldn't see our navigation lights? I switched on the VHF radio.

"Unidentified vessel heading in a northerly direction. We are a small craft in the vicinity, with limited ability to manoeuvre. Come back. Over."

No response.

I tried again. Nothing.

"*Fuck*," I whispered. This was starting to give me the willies. I stopped pedalling and stood up in the open hatch. Five crewmen were clearly visible under the deck lights, working the catch beneath huge outriggers and swinging nets. A trawler!

A wave of panic swept through me. The craft was much smaller than I'd previously thought, and much closer. Worse still, we were on collision course.

What to do? My mind screamed in confusion. Wake Steve? *No, by the time he scrambles out of the Rathole, they'll be on us…* Set off a flare? *No, by the time I locate one in the dark, it'll be too late…*

The fishing boat was now just two hundred yards away and closing fast. There was still time to pedal out of the way, but without two masthead lights to line up one above the other, it was impossible to tell if the vessel was actually going to hit us, or might pass a shade ahead or astern. Pedalling forward or backwards might inadvertently put *Moksha* in its path.

In the end, I did nothing. I just sat there like a deer caught in the headlights. The sound of engines rose in crescendo. The blinding deck lights washed away all remaining vision. Resignation had set in, as if this was the way it was meant to be. The End wasn't the dramatic event I'd always assumed it would be. No terrified close-ups like in the movies. No crashing music in the background. In real life, that interval between living and dying seemed quite normal, even serene.

I braced for impact.

A dark mass towered overhead, the registration number burning into my retinas. My ears filled with the sickening hiss of the bow wave.

Then it was gone. No splintering wood. No churning propellers. The yellow dungaree-clad crewmen out on deck passed so close I could spit on them. Glancing up at the bridge, I saw that it was unmanned. No one was actually driving the thing.

Paralyzed with shock, I sat watching the trawler's white stern light disappear into the night. Eventually, my hands stopped shaking enough to fill the kettle. *Hot tea, yes, that'll help...*

I looked at my watch. It was past three o'clock. Time to wake Steve.

"Just had a close call," I mumbled as he levered himself out of the Rathole. I tried to make it sound casual, but the wavering in my voice betrayed me. I already knew what his reaction would be.

"Why didn't you wake me?" he snapped. "We could've been killed!"

"I thought it was..."—I was stammering now—"farther away than it was. Next thing I looked up and it was right there, heading straight for us. I panicked, and the whole situation sort of... spun out of control. I didn't want to wake you just in time to die."

Steve stared at the bottom of the boat, processing the gravity of what had just happened.

"Next time Jason, *please* wake me up—regardless. I could've been looking for flares while you pedalled."

He was right, of course. For once, I bit my tongue and slipped into the still-warm sleeping compartment without a word, reflecting on how I might handle a shit-hitting-the-fan session next time. I'd never faced a near-death experience before. First time around, I'd completely lost my head.

Little did I realize how soon I'd get a chance to redeem myself.

———— ᴓᴓᴓ ————

THE NEXT DAY a wave flopped into the cockpit unannounced, rendering our video camera inoperable. Reluctant to submit his high-end machine to the rigours of a marine environment, Kenny had managed to borrow an ancient SVHS camcorder from a fellow filmmaker. After nearly a decade of abuse on Whitbread Round the World yacht races, the camera was now so out of date and generally buggered it belonged in a museum. But it was all we had, and with no other means of recording for the documentary series that Kenny had already worked so hard on, we agreed the dutiful thing was to alter course for the island of Madeira to see if we could get the wretched thing fixed.

We'd pedalled 350 miles since leaving Lagos. Up until now, the conditions had been kind, the wind never blowing more than force 4 (fifteen miles per hour). Then, at daybreak on the twelfth morning, just sixty-five miles from Madeira's northern tip, I awoke after three blissful hours in the Rathole to fifteen-foot rollers breaking over the bow. This was *Moksha's* first real test in heavy seas. Would she stay upright?

"Wind's veered and coming from the south," grumbled Steve, his legs straining visibly with the extra effort of pedalling into the wind. "Knees are killing me!"

I dragged myself out of the cosy sleeping bag like a reluctant moth from its cocoon, and perched on the passenger seat, squinting at the ocean. Foaming locks of white spume were streaking from the manes of white horses as far as the eye could see. Life aboard was no longer a tranquil affair. Everything inside was drenched from water crashing over the side, and my Shimano SPD sandals were swimming in several inches of water. Worse still, my last piece of clean clothing, a black and white striped tee shirt I'd clipped to a makeshift clothesline strung from the radar antenna stick, had disappeared.

I swore quietly under my breath. *Bloody. Shit. Fuck. Bollocks.* This Big Wet Bike Ride was turning out to be more than I'd bargained for.

Human voices interrupted my private tirade. With the memory of the near fatal collision still fresh, I leapt to my feet and began anxiously scanning the horizon. There, just a hundred yards astern and approaching at speed, was an off-white motorboat carrying eight orange survival suits shouting and waving in our direction.

"Who the hell are these guys?" said Steve, craning to get a better look.

An enormous container ship to the east, the homeport of MANILA registered on its stern, offered the most likely explanation.

"Filipinos" I replied. "Maybe they think we need rescuing?"

Sure enough, the launch cut its engine twenty yards from our port beam, and a row of short stubby arms beckoned us to come alongside. The orange survival suit at the helm was beaming in triumph.

"We saving you!" it shouted. "We saving you!"

Steve was now standing beside me in the cockpit. "Thanks," he replied, "but we don't need any help."

More gesticulating. More excited chatter celebrating the sensational rescue.

I turned to Steve. "I don't think they understood a word you just said."

He cupped his hands around his mouth and tried again. "WE WANT TO BE HERE. WE DON'T NEED RESCUING, THANK YOU!"

This time the message seemed to hit home. The expressions of our valiant saviours turned from one of victory to utter bewilderment. Another half-hearted bout of arm waving, and they finally gave up, gunning their outboard engine to life and making a beeline back to the mother ship, shaking their heads as they went.

"They must think we're daffy," I chuckled.

"Yep," Steve agreed. "A couple of half-naked nutters bobbing about in a broom cupboard hundreds of miles from anywhere. Difficult to explain in any language."

Our VHF radio sprang to life. It was the skipper of the container ship wanting to clarify his crew's understanding of the situation before taking off. His English was broken, but at least intelligible.

"You no engine?" he asked.

Steve clicked the mouthpiece. "Correct." He had more than a pinch of pride in his voice. "Our vessel is powered by a bicycle. We're pedalling from Europe to America without a sail or a motor. Over."

There was a long pause.

"So we no rescue you?"

"That's affirmative Captain. We do not need rescuing. We appreciate your concern, though."

Another pause.

"One lass question. Which nationality you?"

"English."

"Ah, oh-kay. I am understanding now."

MADEIRA'S VOLCANIC STUB hovered tantalizingly on the horizon for the next two days before the southerly headwind subsided enough for us to make headway again, and close the remaining ten miles to the Port of Funchal. We'd been at sea for only two weeks, but even a glimpse of greenery gave the impression of arriving in paradise. Cars, miniaturized from a mile out, zipped along a waterfront underlining a backdrop of red and white terracotta roofs, the houses set like coral jewels in a lavish mountain crown of luxuriant vegetation sweeping high into the clouds.

We nosed our way into the marina, passing neat rows of elegant snow-white yachts from around the world, their halyards pinging against the masts in the morning breeze. The skipper of a luxury yacht bearing the French flag eyed us suspiciously, no doubt wondering what this ugly *Rosbif* duckling was doing entering such an exclusive marina.

After tying up to the visitors' wharf, Steve wobbled off on his sea legs in search of the harbour office to arrange a more permanent mooring. We had the equivalent of just two pounds sterling in Portuguese escudos between us. By necessity, we were back on the make.

Ten minutes later, he was back with disappointing news. We could only stay an hour where we were before required to exit the harbour and drop anchor in the exposed swell. This posed a problem. We'd forgotten to bring an anchor.

"We could probably snug up alongside that bloody great thing over there without them even noticing," Steve suggested, nodding toward the French gin palace.

"I wouldn't count on it," I replied. "Did you see the look on that frog's face when we came in?"

With a little time to mull over our mooring dilemma, we split up to run essential errands. Steve volunteered to send a fax to our families, letting them know we were still alive, and the reason for the unplanned stopover. I would hit up the local TV station to see if we could get our sick video camera fixed.

We reconvened forty-five minutes later. I had Marina Figueiroa, anchor for the local television station, and a camera operator in tow. A reporter from the Associated Press had also turned up, alerted by the harbour office. With the prospect of a report on the evening news and a full-page spread in next morning's paper, our fortunes began to change.* A complimentary berth magically became available, and donations started to trickle in from a crowd of interested bystanders. In less than one hour, our status had elevated from that of visiting pariahs

---

*   Working the local media to our advantage was something we honed to a fine art over the years. Without their endorsement, we were just a couple of scruffy nobodies rolling up in a new town with a hare-brained idea. A few newspaper articles and a television report later, however, and people's attitudes towards us changed dramatically. Institutions they admired and trusted had sanctioned the "crazy idea," and they suddenly became willing to help in any way they could.

to local celebrities. The TV station technician was taking a look at our camera. The nearby Marina Terrace Fish Restaurant even offered to feed us leftovers after closing time.

As evening fell, our newfound friends and admirers began meandering back to their homes and families. The wind was picking up again from the south, and the sky bruised with a gathering storm. Relinquishing the Rathole to Steve, I wandered off in search of alternative accommodations. A hotel was out of the question. Even the youth hostel was way out of my league at eight quid.

On Avenida Zarco I bought a plastic bottle of gut-rot wine from a supermarket. At least soused, I'd get *some* sleep if I ended up having to doss out in the open. The stuff tasted like gasoline, but did the trick, running down my gullet like molten lava and igniting my belly with fire. A low grumble of thunder rolled in from the darkening mountains, and the first spots of rain sliced across my face like hot embers.

Funchal was now a dead town, deserted streets blubbing with rain. A car hurtled past throwing up sheets of water, the driver straining at the blurred windscreen. The booze started to kick in and I was soaked to the skin, relishing the free shower but stumbling around in danger of being struck by lightning. I threw my head back and laughed, a mad, racking, devil-may-care laugh.

"We showed you, you fuckers!" I shouted, swinging the bottle at all the nay-saying bastards who'd taken one look at *Moksha* and predicted she wouldn't last a day. "We survived! *We fucking well survived!*"

A dog appeared, barking, lunging at my heels. I stepped into a restaurant just in time.

CRASH! A blinding flash of light. Then the lights went out.

"Coooweee!" whooped the locals at the bar, used to the anonymity sprung by frequent power failures.

"Oh my!" cried the tourists at their fancy tables, sitting bolt upright like they had sticks up their arses.

A uniformed waiter blocked my path. "Zorry zir. Power eez kaput! No more zervis tonight." It was a thinly disguised attempt to get rid of me.

"No shit," I slurred, and lurched back into the swirling rain. We'd been out in that damn boat for a fortnight, pedalling around the clock like crazed lunatics, and my first night on land I had nowhere to go.

After an hour of checking out doorways, I arrived at a six-foot-high fence flanking the botanical gardens. Taking hold of the top rung, I heaved myself up and over the spikes.

A narrow concrete path led around a small lake. The place was empty and eerily silent. Out of the darkness, a shelter the size of a large dog kennel appeared. *What kind of animal lives here?* I wondered.

The faint sound of honking reached me. *Ducks! They shouldn't be a problem...*

"Right you lot," I announced, poking my head through the narrow entrance, "Push over. You've got a new roommate."

Dark shapes advanced from the shadows, hissing and spitting aggressively.

These weren't ducks. They were swans! Rottweilers with wings more like it. Beating a hasty retreat was the sensible option, but I was cold, wet, and shivering uncontrollably. Hypothermia would soon set in.

"C'mon you buggers," I pleaded. "You're supposed to like being wet."

Taking a deep breath, I charged headlong into the darkness, slipped, and landed in a pile of shit. The swans shot around and over me in a cacophony of shrieking and madly beating wings, leaving me covered in a thin layer of green manure. No matter. I had a stable, non-moving surface all to myself, something I'd been fantasizing about since leaving Lagos. By the time my head hit the *merda,* I was asleep.

THE UNPLANNED STOPOVER of a few days extended to a week while we waited for parts to be flown in for the camera. It was a happy week, borrowed from that secret reserve of hours, minutes and seconds which occasionally, and for no apparent reason, graces one's otherwise prede-termined life with a little spontaneity and magic.

The delay was also a blessing in disguise. A chance inspection of *Moksha's* underside revealed an eight-inch crack in the skeg, there to hold the propeller shaft in place. If the camera hadn't failed and we'd bypassed Madeira, it would have only been a matter of weeks before the dagger-shaped section of sandwiched timber split completely, and the unsecured shaft dropped to the ocean floor. Without a spare, the only other mode of propulsion was the emergency oars—a dire pros-pect. *Moksha* was too narrow to be rowed for any real distance; enough to avoid shipwreck, but not all the way to Miami.

With time on my hands, I turned my attention to Thoreau's truth, and a simple philosophy for living life on an overpopulated planet. The best place to start, I decided, was within myself. "The man whom God loves is the onion with a million skins," Henry Miller once mused. "To shed the first layer is painful beyond words; the next layer is less painful, the next less still…"

Far from society's tumult and distorting hall of mirrors, the extreme wilderness of the Atlantic Ocean offered the ideal laboratory for such a dismantling process of human consciousness, supplying the solitude and tranquillity needed to peel away the layers and answer the first question:

Who or what am I really?

Meditation would be the means. Each morning I awoke at dawn, and sat cross-legged in the entrance to the swan house. Eyes closed, atten-tion focused on the sensation of cold air flowing in through the nostrils and warm air flowing out, I strove to mimic the posture and breathing technique prescribed in David Fontana's *Elements of Meditation*. The aim was to attain One Pointed Attention, in which the mind advanced from its habitual slavery to mental chatter—the "monkey mind" as the book called it—to a more useful, focused tool in the handling of thought processes.

After nearly a week of diligent practise, I was still useless at it. A few seconds of vague concentration and my attention would be carted off on a merry dance by a disinterested mind skipping along a trail of associations that ultimately led nowhere. Or, I'd fall asleep. Like any new discipline, it was going to take practise and patience—lots of patience. I resolved to continue my efforts on the voyage.

By the tenth morning, repairs to both camera and *Moksha* were complete, and it was time to leave. Fresh supplies from the open-air fruit and vegetable market were stowed on board. We'd even had time to visit a couple of local schools the day before.

I would miss the botanical gardens, its broken windmill with only half the light bulbs working, the folks from the Marina Terrace Restaurant, the custard dumplings from the bakery, and our foxy newsreader popping down to see us every day.

Crawling out of the swan house for the last time, my eyes came to rest on a pair of boots on the grass in front of me. They were connected to a pair of blue trousers, matching jacket, and white shirt containing a short fat man with a bushy black moustache, the dead hamster variety favoured by Portuguese men. He was furious. Using a litter stick for punctuation, the warden of the botanical gardens began machine-gunning me in an unbroken tirade of Portuguese.

"*Youfuckingtouristsyouthinkyoucandowhateverthefuckyoulikewhenyouvisitsomeoneelsescountry, eh?*"

"Okay, okay." I held up my hands in defence. "I'm leaving. I won't be coming back to your swan house, I promise."

"Eef you com 'ere too-nite, I poot you in da rat house!" He grinned triumphantly, delighting at his own wit.

"I suppose that's where you live is it?"

He raised his stick to clobber me, but I was already gone, pegging it back down the path towards the harbour. We had a high tide to catch, and as usual, I was late.

PEDALLING DUE SOUTH from Funchal, we cleared the southern tip of the island and turned southwest. We were now bound for the northeast trades, a belt of reliable winds beginning a few hundred miles off the African coast, blowing fifteen to twenty-five knots all the way to the Caribbean. If we could reach these before being swept too far south by the Canary Current, we had a better than average chance of making it the remaining distance to Miami. Otherwise, we ran the risk of ending up in Central or South America, throwing a major spanner in our circumnavigation plans.

Despite only lasting an hour, our sea trials in Salcombe had alerted us to how pedalling across the Atlantic was likely to be tedious as hell. The truth of it, as we were now finding out, was even worse than that. As fast as Madeira slipped beneath the waves, an all-consuming state of drudgery set in. We became lobotomized hamsters chained to a wheel that constantly needed turning. And the less it turned, the greater the probability of running out of food, or something else going wrong, and the voyage failing.

This kernel of wisdom had been imparted to us in London by the legendary ocean rower Peter Bird during a visit to help fit a ventilation hatch in *Moksha's* roof.

"This central compartment should protect you from the elements nicely," Peter said cheerfully, cutting a hole for the vent above the pedal seat—it leaked like a sieve the entire crossing. "The basic rule of thumb," he continued, "with rowing boats at least, is the less time spent on the water, the better your chances of survival."

His theory was cruelly proven two years later. Sixty-nine days into Peter's fifth attempt to row the Pacific, a signal was picked up by the Russian Rescue Centre in Vladivostok from his water-activated Emergency Positioning Indicating Radio Beacon (EPIRB). When *Sector Two* was found drifting upside down by a passing freighter, it showed all the hallmarks of being rammed by another ship. Either that, or collision with one of the large pieces of timber found floating nearby. Peter's body was never recovered.

Human powering oneself across something as unimaginably vast as one of the world's oceans is less physical as it is a mental challenge. The body is capable of immense feats of endurance, but only if the mind buys into it. Without motivation, our legs were useless. But how to sustain enthusiasm when your target, in our case Miami, is so far away, and the process of getting to it so interminably dull?

We differed on how best to tackle this. Admittedly, Steve, being in charge of navigation, could never hope to escape the constant reminders of our agonizingly slow progress delineated by tiny pencil dots on the chart. His moods, therefore, often mirrored these 24-hour latitude/longitude fixes, and the gaps between them. The wider apart, the happier he was. The closer together, sometimes barely showing even a few miles made good, the more disheartened.

Having responsibilities other than navigation, I was free to occupy my mind with other things. Not that our overall progress wasn't of any concern. Packing enough food had been my duty, after all, and the calculation of ninety ration days was based on the assumption that we could pedal at least forty-five miles per day—a target we often fell short of. But I quickly saw that allowing the proximity of the far shore to dictate morale could bleed the voyage of enjoyment, and in turn affect our physical performance. A slump in spirits triggered by dots closer together would lead to deteriorating performance, and the gaps shrinking still further. Peter's catch-22 would surely kick in.

Besides, was it possible to get something out of the voyage other than just completing it? Perhaps adapt to what was ostensibly a sterile and lifeless desert, tailoring a lifestyle as fulfilling and enjoyable as that on land? Raising Miami would certainly be a tremendous achievement, but could I feel the same sense of regret leaving this alien world of shifting blue as I did watching the familiar solid one of Portugal disappear all those weeks ago? Not if I remain in land mode, I told myself.

And so, a week out from Funchal, I made a conscious decision to forget about Miami, indeed forget about land altogether, turning my attention to the present instead. We were already using little incentives set at regular intervals to motivate ourselves towards. A three-hour shift between one and four in the morning, for example, might be rewarded with a cup of tea and a chocolate bar. And every three hundred miles, or five degrees of longitude marked as a vertical black line on the chart, we congratulated ourselves with a swig of Ballantine's whiskey. But these enticements weren't always enough. The more tired and fed up we became, the less effective traditional goal setting. The distance was just too far, and the psychological carrots too few and far between.

There were no tricks to call on from our former land lives, either. The means by which Western society drives performance, consumer-related criteria such as money, career, mortgage, designer labels, retirement fund, Christmas bonus, credit rating, and so on, meant nothing in the oceanic wilderness.

A completely new set of values was called for to inhabit this liquid world effectively, and provide a framework for motivation to cross it as quickly as possible. All that I formerly held to be solid and true needed to be put under the microscope. Only then could I hope to build a constructive relationship with the sea, and begin to address those complexities of the mind that had dogged me for so long.

———⟨⟨⟨———

November 15. Day 29

1:00 am. There are many God-awful things that I've come to tolerate on this boat, but getting up at all hours of the night to pedal for three hours will never be one of them.

4:00 am. Just finished first graveyard shift—a real killer. Like motorway driving at night when you're dog-tired, except worse. Head slumping forward every few minutes, then whipping back and smacking against the stern window.

(Journal)

LONG-TERM FATIGUE, or Creeping Grey Funk as we called it, became an evil thing lurking in the shadowy recesses of our sleep-deprived minds, waiting to crawl in and feed as exhaustion grew. Slowly, imperceptibly, it wound its way like a parasite into every aspect of our lives, lessening our ability to execute tasks safely, and stealing even the tiniest scrap of pleasure from things we once enjoyed, like reading a book, or cooking a meal. The rigid shift system was becoming a double-edged sword. The same discipline that kept the pedals turning 24/7, and the boat from drifting off course, allowed for only three hours of sleep at a time, and never more than five in any 24-hour period. After a fortnight of this, we were turning into the living dead.

Steve suggested we break up the hamster routine by doing a little fishing. On Madeira, we'd been befriended by Heinz, a boozy old salt with ivory beard and bushy eyebrows. A former U-boat commander, Heinz made it his business to show up every morning and pick holes in our preparations for the big crossing. The other annoying habit he had was to bang on about fishing.

"Vat are you doingk for zer fees?" he asked for the umpteenth time on the penultimate morning of departure.

Our response was always the same: "We're not going to bother Heinz. We have all the food we need."

"But you must fees to survive! You must fees to survive!"

On any other morning, he would chant this as a mantra until we either found a way of getting rid of the old bastard or fleeing ourselves. Today, however, he reached into his jacket pocket, and pulled out a roll of stout marlin line and a thumb-sized lure carved from wood. Furnished with eye-catching tassels at one end, it was, according to Heinz, "Guaranteed to catch more fees zan you know vot to do viz!"

We'd been trolling Lolita the Lure (so nicknamed) for an hour a day since leaving Madeira, and caught not a damn thing. The result of each day's effort was so predictable it had become a running joke. "You hungry?" Steve would ask, pulling in the line. "Let's see what Lolita has caught us for dinner tonight shall we?"

Something had to change. Lolita needed a makeover.

Using red and black felt-tip pens, I gave Lolita a pair of exotic Cleopatra eyes and sassy smile. Provocatively curled Betty Boop eyelashes completed the picture of sex appeal—although, as Steve pointed out, the idea was to get the fish to swallow the lure, not have sex with it.

Whatever. Within a minute of throwing out the all-new pimped-out Lolita, the line strained to its limit, and a huge dorado fish soared into the air twenty yards astern. All hell immediately broke loose. The inside of the boat erupted into a melee of shouting, swearing, and shrieks of delight as we pulled the gasping beast alongside. The challenge was now to land the thing without it flipping off the hook. Retrieving the old sail bag we'd used to store our Madeiran veggies, I jumped into the water.

My plan was to scoop the fish into the bag, which Steve could then haul aboard. The fish, not surprisingly, had other ideas. As soon as it saw me, it shot under the boat, and started winding itself plus the monofilament line round and round the propeller.

Events then took an unexpected turn. What started out as a harmless bit of fun spiraled rapidly out of control...

The sail bag had slipped from my fingers during the confusion, and was slowly drifting upwind. Or, to be precise, the bag remained stationary in the water while *Moksha* and I were blown downwind. I started to swim towards the bag. "I'll just go and grab it," I yelled.

"You sure it's worth it?" Steve shouted after me.

I pretended not to hear, and kept swimming. *Damn Steve*, I thought irritably, *being a safety officer as usual*. After all, the bag was only a few feet away.

But by the time I reached it, *Moksha* was already sixty feet downwind, pushed by the wind and the waves.

On the long slog back, swimming breaststroke with the bag around my neck, I tired easily. With our legs doing all the pedalling, our upper bodies had lost what little conditioning they'd had on land. A wave broke suddenly from behind, filling my nose and throat with saltwater. I stopped to cough out the brine, losing valuable seconds as I trod water. When I resumed my stroke, I looked up and saw the boat even farther downwind. This was alarming. *Moksha* was drifting faster than I could swim.

There's nothing for it. Steve will have to come back and get me…

He was sitting on the stern, anxiously watching my progress. Somehow he'd managed to retrieve the fish from the water and had it clasped tight to his chest. Now I'd have to suffer the ignominy of hearing him say, "I told you so!"

"Steve!" I shouted. "I think I'm in trouble!"

His mouth opened and closed, but the words were taken by the wind. I was about to call out again when my throat froze with a terrible realization.

The fishing line… fouled around the propeller…

In the time it took for him to rummage in the stern compartment for a mask and a knife, go overboard and cut the tangle free, then clamber back in and turn *Moksha* around, we'd be completely separated.

Shit! I'll have to make it back myself, or…

I remembered the story my father once told me of how, as a boy, he'd nearly drowned off the beach at West Bay in Dorset. After the initial frantic struggle, he described the sensation as being almost pleasurable, "like falling into a trance." My grandfather, watching from shore, ran in and dragged him out just in time.

Another surprise wave broke from behind, flooding my lungs a second time. As I fought for air, what I took to be the same woozy sensation began spreading throughout my body. Blood was thumping against my eardrums. Nothing seemed to matter anymore. Like the near miss with the trawler, that interface between light and dark, life and death, seemed perfectly normal, as if this was the way it was meant to be.

My arms grew steadily weaker, and my stroke more erratic. I should have known hypoxia was kicking in when the sky turned the colour of red wine and the water around me black ink, as though saturated with blood.* *From the dying dorado,* I thought deliriously. Sharks sprang to mind. *The smell of blood will attract them, whip them into a feeding frenzy...*

At that moment, something tripped in my consciousness. While the idea of drowning seemed tolerable, almost pleasant, being eaten alive by sharks most certainly did not. The soporific state of quiet surrender vanished, replaced by a primal urge to live welling up from the innermost depths of my being. And with it came reality hurtling back into sharp focus.

I began swimming for my life. My arms were screaming, but I knew that keeping sight of Steve between the towering crests was the only hope I had. Waves were breaking from behind, one after the other. Frothy sputum whipped from the crests, blurring my vision. *Moksha* slowly slipped from view. As the seconds turned into minutes, I no longer knew whether I was making progress, or even heading in the right direction. The only thing that kept my spent arms turning was

---

* Hypoxia: oxygen starvation to the body's tissues, including the brain, leading to headaches, fatigue, shortness of breath, euphoria, and hallucinations.

the certainty that sharks were closing in. Any second I would feel razor-sharp teeth tearing into my flesh...

In those final seconds of hopelessness and despair, going on as if for eternity, the fingers of my right hand collided with something solid. I felt my wrist being grabbed—Steve heaving me on deck. When all seemed lost, I imagined a divine hand reaching out and offering me my life back.

Slumped on the stern deck, gasping for breath, my eyes met the gaze of the dying dorado, its silent suffocation all too poignant.

ALTHOUGH BEGINNING TO see progress with short meditation sessions snatched during my graveyard shifts, I felt the need for more direct, hands-on exercises to explore the mechanics of consciousness during daylight hours.

Holding a length of twine in each hand and balancing Richard Hopkins's *Pocket Guide to Knots* on my knees, I first re-learned how to tie a bowline, a clove hitch, and a sheet bend, essential knots my father taught me years ago. Each knot I first tied according to the illustrations before dissecting. More than just learning rote, I wanted to understand the way the knot worked, the relationship of the surfaces and how they operated in different planes of movement to produce friction and a tight hold that wouldn't slip.

The bowline, for example, is a relatively straightforward knot picked up in a few minutes. Used typically to create a fixed loop at the end of a rope, I thought I had the prescribed technique licked until a fatal flaw came to light: having to use both hands to tighten, making the knot too dangerous to tie out on deck in heavy seas. It took a full two hours to strip the whole thing down and customize a new technique that could be tightened one-handed. The result was so familiar, and the tying of it so second nature, that I was willing to stake both our lives on it.

One interesting by-product of tying a knot this way was how time seemed to disappear. I applied the same approach to a variety of other chores that, at least at first glance, offered little if any satisfaction in doing them: cleaning out the crud from the food lockers, sewing torn clothes, pumping water, even pedalling itself. The secret was immersion in the present, in the very act of doing. And the more I persevered at these menial tasks without thought of past, future, or the end result, the greater the sense of fulfilment.

In each case, a seamless interaction emerged, dissolving the division between subject and object, until all awareness of independent "self" performing the task, or the external object being acted upon, ceased to be. Sense of time fell away as the two melded as one. It was like driving a car and remembering nothing of the journey. Yet, somehow, you used a highly sophisticated machine to perform a series of complex manoeuvres over many miles without being consciously aware of it.

Aboard *Moksha*, there was another benefit to this synthesis. Whether it was sewing a torn tee shirt, repairing the hot chocolate mug, or simply pedalling, the outcome would always be of a higher standard than if I rattled off the job just to get it done.

I called these Created Value tasks in my journal.

Sometimes, however, fatigue would either kick in, or I just couldn't be bothered to begin the process. On these occasions it was easier to fall back on activities that were the result of someone else's efforts. When my head began to loll during the second graveyard shift, I would stick on the headphones and crank up Radiohead's *Pablo Honey*, or *Last Splash* by The Breeders. In the day, I might open a packet of "fly sandwiches," the army issue snack of currents squashed between two oblong biscuits, or pick out a light read from our mobile library of books.* These I termed Acquired Value acts, as they required the minimum of mental

---

* We miscalculated on the Atlantic voyage, taking too many books on philosophy and human awareness. Most of the time all we felt like reading were trashy novels and comics.

effort and creativity, the equivalent of vegging in front of the TV at the end of a hard workday.

There was one major drawback to Acquired Value acts. Like any pleasure derived from the senses, the distraction was short-lived. The mind, like a hungry baby, always cried for more. Unlike the longer-term satisfaction supplied by Created Value events, Acquired Value ones were little more than a quick fix.

BY NOVEMBER 29, day forty-three, we'd been at sea long enough for the mystery boils we'd been warned of to start appearing. These were the devils own creation, painful sores leaking a steady stream of pus caused by prolonged exposure to saltwater. Steve had one on his backside the size of a hen's egg. I had little sympathy, having watched him pick it for the past week.

The added discomfort made us all the more irritable. Friction began mounting over a catalogue of annoyances we unwittingly supplied each other. As I scribbled angrily in my journal:

Steve's antisocial traits include but are not limited to: never cleaning the hot chocolate mug after using it; using my sweat towel without asking—as well as being unhygienic, it now smells like old rabbits; farting indiscriminately at mealtimes.

Bottom-line he's really, really getting on my tits!

His journal was no doubt filled with similar entries about me.

As THE DAYS rolled into weeks and the weeks into months, the notion of man-made time gradually faded, as Rimauld from Orléans said it would. The increments on our watches were still essential to navigation and metering out fairly portioned pedal shifts. For all other points of reference, however, including our sense of orientation within the four-dimensional space-time continuum—our Cosmic Suspension Fix as we called it—we found ourselves gravitating towards the age-old time-keepers of the universe, the stars and planets gliding silently across the night sky, and the sun arcing above us in the day. To keep track of how long we'd been out there, we took it in turns carving a single Robinson Crusoe-style notch into the cabin timbers every sunrise.

Some nights the ocean would lull to a murmur and, while Steve slept, I would take a break from pedalling to boil water for a mug of hot chocolate, then stand in the hatchway, head cocked back, gazing far into the belly of the universe with mute admiration. The major constellations and notable stars—Taurus, Leo, Sirius, Canis Major, Gemini, Cassiopeia, and, of course, Polaris—became my night-time companions. With no light pollution from human habitation, no mountains, buildings, trees or any other obstacle between the horizons, sometimes the tapestry of the night sky became so heavily pregnant with swathes of tiny pinpricks, swirling and layering one upon the other, that all there seemed to *be* was light, with no darkness in there at all, and the sky might collapse at any moment with the sheer burden of carrying it all.

These were some of the most remarkable moments to be alive when, if I stared long enough, a sense of ultimate equilibrium would permeate throughout my being, like celestial kinaesthesia. And I imagined Peter up there, still plugging away on his final voyage, threading his little rowboat between the islands of the Milky Way, a journey without end through the watery vastness of space...

Then my neck would start to ache, and the pedals would cry out to be turned once more.

Unfortunately, the night of December 5 was not one of those idyllic nights. A few days before we'd at last sighted the fabled puffball clouds of the trade winds. A storm passing to the south added to the wind speed, whipping the sea into a barging mass of clumsy twenty-five-foot rollers. The first time I stared into the trough of one of these things, I thought we were done for. Surely, our tiny boat would be engulfed! The giant towered briefly overhead, and in the next instant we were on top of it, gazing in awe across the cavernous valley to the next peak. Up and down *Moksha* rode the backs of these leviathans like a flea clinging to the rump of a bucking bull. Instead of resisting the power of the sea like a larger vessel would, she behaved like a cork, going with the flow. Her response to every twitch and nuance of the ocean skin was so immediate, and so transparent, that eventually I, too, came to feel a part of the ocean body, and with it more convinced that this tiny bundle of wood and glue might actually make it to the other side.

Before midnight, Steve insisted on throwing out the two old car tyres that served as our poor-man's sea anchor—we hadn't been able to afford the proper parachute type. Tied to a three-hundred-foot length of rope, they brought *Moksha* perpendicular to the waves, lessening the chance of capsizing. The violent whirring of the chain as we hurtled down the front of big waves also made it difficult for Steve to get his head down being the lighter sleeper. Exhaustion was mounting, and we were nearing the point of being unable to operate the boat safely. Proper rest was needed, even if it meant the boat drifting.

At the same time, it was maddening not to take advantage of the favourable conditions. After weeks of blowing from all directions, the wind had suddenly veered in our favour, allowing us to make significant headway west. Now was the time to make hay, I argued. Steve disagreed. As he pointed out, without sleep there might not be anyone to make the hay if we lost control of the boat and flipped.

Infuriated, I told Steve he could take the Rathole for the entire night. *If he's that tired,* I thought, *let him have the whole damn thing to himself!* I tried catnapping in the pedal seat, leaning forward with my head resting on my arms, but it was impossible. *Moksha* rolled so violently it felt like my head was going to snap off. I tried lying curled around the pedal system instead, but several inches of water sloshing in the bilges made it equally hellish.

Idiot! This is what you get for your pig-headed pride...

The last resort was the stern compartment. There was just enough room to squeeze in between the roof and our bags of non-biodegradable rubbish. It was like sleeping at the municipal dump, bin liners filled with dirty tins and soiled food sachets starting to rot, smelling horribly. But it was dry, and vaguely horizontal.

THE NEXT MORNING I was more exhausted than ever. Five sleepless hours wrestling bags of refuse and being tossed around in a giant tumble dryer made all the other discomforts of the voyage seem like birthday treats. Steve looked fresh as a daisy by comparison. A full night of uninterrupted sleep had had a miraculous effect. Silently, I seethed. Not so much at Steve for pulling rank over the sea anchor, but at myself for playing the martyr card and surrendering the Rathole so easily.

Self-admonishment aside, relations between Steve and I were now so strained the sum total of words used in our daily conversation could be counted on two hands.

"Pass the salt."

"Here you go."

The straw that broke the camel's back was the way in which we did our laundry, on the morning of day forty-nine.

In the absence of both hot water and detergent, we'd developed a rudimentary washing technique that involved lathering our few remaining garments with dish soap, then tying them into a crude bundle and towing them behind the boat for an hour or so. This made little difference to how filthy they were, but even going through the motions of exorcising grime made us feel a little more on top of things psychologically. Hygiene, or at least the notion of it, was vital. Once this started to go, it was a short, slippery slope of hopelessness and despair, leading to a festering mire of insanity. We didn't want to become known as *"those two guys found pedalling in circles a thousand miles off the coast of Africa, doodling with their own poo."*

As the voyage progressed, I'd unintentionally left my laundry out a little longer each time, until forgetting about it altogether. The first I knew of this was Steve pulling the sodden bundle aboard and thrusting it accusingly in my face.

"You realize we've been dragging this for three whole days, don't you Jason."

"Are you asking or telling?" I replied defiantly.

"Well, you have. And I've worked something out. That towing your clothes for seventy-two hours with a quarter of a knot's drag has added nearly twelve miles to the voyage. We spent *days* sanding the hull to get the boat to glide through the water with the minimum of friction. Now I don't know why we even bothered!"

Is the bastard being serious? I thought.

Steve was highly intelligent, and a master at reasoned argument. Not having the same way with words, I usually tackled his fancy dialectic footwork by going into a sulk. This time, however, I knew he was baiting me. Withering sarcasm was called for instead.

"Well that's funny," I said. "Because I also worked something out. At this speed, in the salinity of seawater at this latitude, it takes *exactly* three days to clean the skid marks out of a pair of underpants."

"Bollocks!" Steve spat. "That really is a load of bollocks, Jason. And you know it!"

The gloves were off, and the laundry instantly forgotten. All the petty grievances building over the days and weeks came spewing to the surface: Steve never cleaning the hot chocolate mug, the way I shuffled into my sandals, Steve's indiscriminate farting, how I blew my nose by pinching it between thumb and forefinger. Our voices rose in a spiralling duet of vitriolic diatribes until we came the nearest to physical blows since leaving Greenwich.

Such annoyances, so infinitesimal as to hardly be worth acknowledging on land, became incidents worthy of UN intervention at sea. What we didn't realize at the time, of course, was how the situation we'd chosen for ourselves, a floating torture chamber, set us against each other. The nearest either of us came to "getting out of the house and going for a walk" was to sit out on the bow every other evening and watch the sun go down. Nature just hadn't intended for humans to live so close together for so long, especially not two twenty-something males with competing egos.

We never communicated our emotions, either. As Brits, we would rather be dragged by wild horses before admitting to even having them. I didn't fully appreciate, therefore, why Steve got so antsy about leaving the hatch open in bad weather. Beneath his steely appearance, he was deeply wary of the sea. And once, when he'd asked me why I insisted on keeping a diving knife beside the bunk in the Rathole, I was too embarrassed to tell him.

Although intimidated by shipping, I felt totally at home on the ocean wave. I wasn't afraid of mountainous seas, or falling overboard. Rather, it was a figment of boyhood imagination, fuelled by Jules Verne's *Twenty Thousand Leagues Under the Sea*, and illustrations in old storybooks of grotesque sea monsters clinging to the sides of stricken square riggers, their giant arms snaking up the masts, plucking terrified sailors out of the rigging like ripened fruit.

The Kraken was a mythical beast from Norwegian legend, large enough to envelop entire ships and drag them to the depths. But these were just tall tales, traceable back to inebriated sailors embellishing their experiences in dockside bars, right?

The giant squid, from which stories of the Kraken were likely drawn, is a very real creature of the *Architeuthidae* family living in all the world's oceans. Growing up to a length of fifty feet, specimens caught in trawler nets off the coast of New Zealand show them equipped with eight arms and two longer tentacles lined with spherical suction cups, one to two inches in diameter, for latching onto prey. It was these same leathery tentacles I imagined reaching into *Moksha's* cockpit in the middle of the night and hoiking us into the water.

Three nights after the laundry bust up, I was sound asleep in the Rathole while Steve took the first graveyard shift: 10:00 pm to 1:00 am. Shortly after midnight, I awoke to the sound of heavy pounding on the underside of the hull.

THUMP! —THUMP! —CRASH! —THUMP!

I peered out of the Rathole. "What the hell was *that?*" I whispered.

Steve had stopped pedalling. His eyes were the size of golf balls. "No idea. Something pretty substant— "

BANG! — CRASH! — THUMP! —THUMP!

The heavy-duty canvas straps holding down the centreboard were straining, the boat shuddering with every blow.

"Why don't you stick your head out and see what it is?" I suggested.

Steve glared at me. "Why don't you stick *your* fucking head out and see what it is?" He reached forward to grab the pair of knotted ropes connected to the sliding hatch. With a sharp tug, he pulled it shut.

Just in time.

Whatever it was must have been huge, lifting the entire boat out of the water. For a moment, it looked like we were going over. *Moksha* rolled to starboard and slid back into the water with a loud splash.

Then everything went quiet. The only sound was my pulse as I held my breath. Steve began slowly pedalling forward. "Maybe it's a container that's fallen off a shi—"

THUMP! —CRASH! —THUMP!

This clearly wasn't the case. Whatever it was, it was very much alive. "Just pedal like fuck!" I cried.

Steve started cranking for all he was worth. Seconds passed. We waited for the final onslaught: the boat capsizing in one almighty heave before the tentacles began working on the bodies in the water.

It never came. Whatever it was had slithered back into the depths. Or maybe it was just a whale with an itchy back?

As CONVERSATION DWINDLED, the world of words became increasingly redundant. Such an intrinsic part of everyday life on land, language on Planet *Moksha* became just another layer of the onion, the conditioned self, to peel away and stick under the microscope for examination.

I wondered whether the same intimacy I'd forged with knot tying and other Created Value tasks might extend to language and the etymology of words. "The trouble with words is that you never know whose mouths they've been in," the English dramatist Dennis Potter once quipped. Some words lent themselves to shared meaning. Others didn't. Were the *meanings* of certain words determined by first-hand *experience* of what they represented?

The English word *dog*, for example, would mean the same thing to any one of a thousand people who'd actually come into contact with one: a warm blooded carnivorous creature equipped with a fur coat, a tail, walking on all fours. Put those same letters back to front, however, and the picture becomes quite different. *God* would likely yield a thousand individual meanings to those same people, if any. Interpretation might range from a bearded bloke sitting on a cloud angrily slinging thunderbolts, to subtle vibrations in the ether, to something that doesn't exist at all.

In each case, the word god represents something personal

and ineffable, unobservable by science and therefore unproven to "exist." If Steve experienced a transcendent state of consciousness aboard *Moksha* and wanted to share it with me, how would he do it? The three letters G, O, and D would be hopelessly misleading, like using a mirage in the desert to pinpoint water. Whereas universal understanding of what "dog" represents is easily achieved through language, an equivalent understanding of "god" is impossible, mere illusion.

How ludicrous, I thought, the pattern throughout history of people fighting, persecuting, and dying for what they perceived these three letters, or the translation in their own language, to mean.

I made a list of other "dirty words," labels so often misused that people assumed they had concrete meaning of their own. Words like, *right, wrong, good, bad, selfish, kind, quality, greatness, best, tolerance, exploit, and falsehood.* During the graveyard shifts, I'd spend an hour or more repeating one of them over and over as I pedalled, until all associations shaped by culture, upbringing, education, religion, the media, and so on, fell away. All that remained would be the empty sounding husk of a word, devoid of fixed meaning. I'd then spend the remainder of the shift examining it objectively in the hope of a more inclusive understanding.

The word "understanding" itself was a good example. As I'd discovered tying bowlines, there are two very different types: the rational method of copying mechanically from people, books, or the Internet, open to anyone, but limited in scope; and the intuitive method that can be adapted to a specific circumstance, but which takes longer to master, and cannot be imitated.

Using modifying adjectives of *rational* and *intuitive* to differentiate between such significant shifts in meaning seemed too clumsy and inadequate. So I did away with the word understanding altogether, and created two symbols in its place.

Over the following weeks and months, I meditated on other dirty words, replacing them with as many ideograms as was necessary to represent the different insights that arose. By the end of the voyage, my journal writing relied heavily upon a new script comprising some one hundred symbols.

None of them would mean anything to anyone else, of course, but that was the point. They were tailored alternatives to words subjected to centuries of abuse, releasing them from the burden of foisting rational, scientific meaning on concepts only truly accessible through direct, personal experience.

December 6

Saltwater sores plague our every waking move. As well as the enormous one on his bottom, Steve has a couple of fresh ones on his left kneecap leaking a steady stream of creamy discharge. I, too, have a huge Mt Etna-like thing on my right forearm that hurt like buggery when I hit it against the bulkhead earlier. Another, already the size of a marble, is bulging from my scrotum... (Journal)

THE EVENING ROUTINE began like any other. At six o'clock we made ready to change positions, a procedure as awkward on this the fiftieth day of the voyage as it was on the first. Coming off his late afternoon shift, Steve flung a sweat-soaked towel to the front of the cabin, and shunted the pedal seat forward to jam a chock of wood behind it, compensating for my shorter legs. Another minute of faffing, and we made the switch, shuffling past each other in the narrow space like two crabs locked in a ritual dance. This almost always resulted in the exiting pedaller, on this occasion Steve, having his calves raked by the serrated teeth of the pedals.

Changeover complete, we settled down to enjoy our favourite part of the day. Following the afternoon roasting, the temperature was now perfect, a light breeze wafting in through the hatch, cooling our tender-ized skin. The setting sun seemed to hover for a moment, then lower its smouldering mass onto a pillow of low-lying clouds that sealed the offing as a grey weld. The western horizon ignited with an iridescent wash of fire stretching far over our heads to the east, and for the next thirty minutes we were treated to one of nature's most well-rehearsed recitals: gentle brushstrokes massaging a canvas of living art from one masterpiece to the next, until the curtain of night finally fell.

Shortly before seven, I switched on the short wave radio. Most eve-nings it was hard to pick up anything now we were 1,500 miles from land. But with the clouds in the west providing a ceiling for the airwaves to bounce off, the BBC World Service sputtered to life. The hourly news from Bush House offered the usual depressing fare: an atrocity by Chechen rebels, Croatian Serb forces shelling Bihac, an oceanographic agreement on the "orderly" exploitation of the oceans.

The only positive note in amongst the usual platter of human mis-ery was Bill Clinton speaking out against Indonesia on the topic of East Timorese self-rule. "I have held the view since 1991," he drawled, "be-fore holding this current term of office, that East Timor should have more of a say in its own affairs."

Flipping the dial, I caught the tail end of Katie Durham's business report for Voice of America. There were eighteen shopping days until Christmas, apparently, and one of the hottest-selling gifts in the USA this holiday season was an expanded polystyrene capital punishment kit.

While I pedalled, despairing of the species, Steve began the evening meal. We were now eating all of our rations, even the six sachets of sugar in each pack, and the sickly packets of Tunes crammed with Vi-tamin C to ward off scurvy. Barry Sadler's dried figs were nearly gone, and we'd decided to eat my mother's homemade Christmas cake early. It made sense to keep as strong as we could, as long as we could, relying on the closeness of land in the latter stages of the voyage to shore up flagging spirits and muscles.

Yet, even consuming more than 8,000 calories each per day, the pounds were still dropping off. The most highly prized psychological carrot of all was the daily Mars Bar. I ate mine quickly. The longer I tried to save it, the louder it called to me from the ration pack. Better to just gobble the thing in one go and be done with it. Steve, on the other hand, consumed his in a highly elaborate fashion: first nibbling away the outer coating of chocolate, then licking off the caramel mid-section, before the tortuous-to-watch finale of sucking the nougat like a lollypop until it was all gone. He became a master of tease, prolonging the process for fifteen minutes or more.

"Ouch! Damn this fucking thing!"

For the umpteenth time, Steve had burnt his fingers trying to light the propane stove with the matchless fire set, a flint and steel worked back and forth until the sparks ignited the gas. Still cursing, he slid a pot of instant mashed potatoes under the bent arm of the stove, and turned his attention to reconstituting two packets of freeze-dried beef granules in the other saucepan.

Ten minutes later, it was ready to dole out. This was the most critical part of meal preparation, carried out on the bottom of the boat in full view of the other person. There was never any question of it being done anywhere else. Even the risk of a wave crashing over the side and ruining the meal was an acceptable price to pay for transparency. To avoid any suspicion I might have of being diddled out of even the tiniest scrap, Steve added an extra spoon of his portion to mine. I would do the same next time I cooked.

Reaching forward, he passed me a steaming plate. It was bland, tasteless muck, but delicious muck nonetheless. And there was never enough of it. We ate in silence, only the sound of scraping spoons filling the space.

"Have you thought about women much?" Steve asked finally.

"Nope," I replied through a mouthful of mash. "Haven't had a stiffy in weeks. Let alone a wank."

We both suffered from Mariner's Droop, a form of erectile dysfunction common to blue water sailors sequestered from sexual intimacy. As a survival mechanism, the brain automatically channelled sex drive to other, more useful tasks.

"Me neither." Steve smirked. "Apart from one I had a few days out from Madeira."

"Really! How did you manage that you sly bugger?"

"During my graveyard shift. You were asleep at the time."

Built along utilitarian lines, with not an extra inch apportioned to comfort, the notion of privacy on board *Moksha* was an abstract one. Even taking a crap was a shared experience, performed in full view of the other.

"Genitals are a waste of space out here anyway," Steve went on. "Other than to pee with."

I nodded. "They just get in the way. Should've had mine surgically removed in Portugal!"

"And stitched back on in Miami?"

"Sure."

"Maybe you should leave it off, Jason. Keep you out of trouble."

"Cheeky fucker."

I looked at my old friend. Apart from a torn red tee shirt and shabby ginger beard, he was naked, as was I. Clothes had ceased to serve any purpose this far from land—there was no one to be offended. Our skin stayed dryer, too, lessening the effects of chaffing. Watching Steve's body rock back and forth in time with the swell, I was struck by how gaunt he looked. His eyes were beginning to glaze. Did I look the same? Probably.

Steve is looking more and more like a worn-out toothbrush, I journaled that evening. *Every day, a few more bristles seem to be missing...*

Pedalling wasn't the only agent of weight loss. The movement of the boat was burning more calories than either of us realized, keeping every muscle in our bodies working constantly to maintain balance. Even so, I was sure Steve was losing condition faster.

Reaching into the starboard food compartment, Steve fished out a packet of freeze-dried apple flakes. Reconstituted with boiling water, the pieces of dried fruit were our favourite dessert. My mouth watered in anticipation.

"Oh no," Steve groaned, turning the bag over and shaking his head. "Martin's jokes are getting worse."

He held it up for me to read. "Jason's dandruff," was scrawled in red marker. While custom packing the rations in London, Martin had written jokes and peppy messages on some of the bags. Though well meaning, his efforts to divert our attention from the discomforts of the voyage only added to the pain and suffering.

Steve opened the bag and wedged it between his thighs. Keeping the top open with his left hand, he proceeded to pour boiling water from the kettle with his right, absorbing each passing wave with his hips.

BOOM! A freak roller slammed into the starboard beam, tipping the bag into his crotch. His face crumpled in agony.

"YEEAAAAAGHHHHHFFFUUUCKKK! WATER! QUICK!"

Jumping to my feet, I reached over the side with the hot chocolate mug, filled it with seawater, and flung the contents at his genitals.

The screams redoubled, attaining an impressive new pitch.

"Not saltwater you fucking idiot! *Freshwater!*"

His Johnson was starting to blister, and his gently steaming balls resembled a pair of microwaved walnuts.

I threw him my water bottle. "Here, use this."

He pulled out the nozzle and squeezed. *Pfffhhhht—* Nothing came out, just an empty fart of air and bubbles. He glowered at me.

I shrugged. "Saltwater will prevent infection. Just try to detach yourself from the pain."

Tears were now rolling down my partner's face. Perhaps this wasn't the right time to start extolling David Fontana's pain control strategies.

"Bugger infection!" Steve bawled, affirming my suspicions. "My fucking bollocks are on fire! For the love of God, freshwater, please…"

Groping under one of the canvas compartment covers, I located the two-and-a-half-gallon container we used to store our drinking water from the desalinator pump. I popped the lid and tipped the can over his groin, releasing a steady stream. Steve's eyes closed in relief.

"Looks like a nuclear power station down there!" I chuckled, nodding at the rising steam.

Strangely, the joke was lost on him.

A few minutes later the container was empty, and three hours of laboriously pumped water was swishing in the bilges. Steve's wedding tackle was still throbbing scarlet. Some other cooling device was urgently needed if the poor bugger ever wanted to start a family.

A stiff easterly breeze offered the solution.

Crawling gingerly out onto the cabin roof, Steve lay back against the car tyres, and pointed his master of ceremonies at Africa.

"Better lash you down so you don't roll overboard," I said, pulling a bungee cord tight across his chest.

Returning to the pedal seat, I resumed pedalling, my crewmate strapped to the top of the boat like a hunting trophy. For the rest of the night I listened to the faint sound of moaning, and for the first time in too long a time I felt ashamed of myself. It was at moments like these that I regained perspective on what was important. Certainly not my petty grievances about whether or not he washed out the hot chocolate mug, or farted like a pig without so much as an "if you please." What mattered was respecting the other person as a fellow human being first, and an expedition partner second.

Tolerance, compassion, and understanding were, after all, qualities the expedition sought to promote as part of its education programme.

What was the good of trying to encourage such attributes in others if I couldn't even find them within myself?

December 13

IRONICALLY, STEVE NUKING his testicles thawed relations between us. The ice really broke a week later when I happened on a bud of Durban Poison, still sticky and pungent, hidden in a matchbox under the canvas bunk. It was a gift from California Carlos to replace Terry's Ships Biscuits—all scoffed in Lagos, of course.

I looked at Steve. "Do we have any rolling papers?"

Like me, he was grinning inanely at the thought of loosening the reins a little. Our cast iron routine had become relentless.*

"No. I'll just rip out a blank page from my journal."

The upshot of mixing in some Lipton's tea and sealing with Bostik adhesive was something more akin to a diseased turnip than a competently rolled joint. But the effects were the same, and whether it was the Bostik or the pot that worked, five minutes later we were both stoned to the boots and sniggering like kids chuffing fags behind the bike sheds. A tendril of smoke curled out through the open cockpit and gathered in a sallow pall over the water, now flat as a millpond.

Our tongues loosened, our brains relaxed, and we ended up having the longest conversation since leaving Portugal.

"What do you miss out here?" Steve asked.

"Oh... family, friends, laughing. You?"

"Definitely family."

---

* We'd been given several bottles of hard liquor in Lagos, but apart from the Ballantine's whiskey we used as a reward for hitting the 5-degree lines of longitude, we never touched any of it. Once "out there," the last thing we felt like doing was losing grip on reality, preferring instead to keep our wits about us 24/7. Being a flat calm day with little chance of anything going wrong, the Durban Poison occasion was a one-off.

I thought for a moment. "What are you looking forward to most when we make landfall?"

"Getting off this fucking boat!"

We laughed. It was just like old times, making us feel almost human again. Steve talked fondly of the Irish girl he'd met at the summer camp in Southern France. Eilbhe's love of simple living, good times, and Celtic music had obviously made a big impression on him. She sounded the quintessential leprechaun, the mischievous complement to the more serious, circumspect Steve.

"I'm thinking of taking up the Irish fiddle!" he said brightly.

"Oh no," I groaned. "Please don't. At least not until we've crossed the Pacific." I explained how I'd taken lessons at school. "But after four years it still sounded like a cat being castrated. And you don't have a musical bone in your body, Steve!"

For the first time we levelled with each other about the voyage, acknowledging the aspects that needled us the most: the lack of emotional stimulus, the restriction of movement. Our spinal muscles had atrophied from all the sitting. Would we even be able to walk once we reached land, we wondered?

Other organs were also suffering from lack of use. Only that morning I'd seen a scorpion fish floating past, adorned with resplendent fins and colourful spines.

"Then I did a double take. Realized it was just a old flip-flop."

We mused at how twisted our perceptions had become, towards each other, and the world around us. Hallucinations too.

"Thought I heard a police siren the other night," Steve said, shaking his head and smiling. "Also a dinner party. I could hear people's conversations, the sound of glasses clinking together for the toast…"

Our sensory spectrum had clearly narrowed. Oceanic colours were reduced to blues, whites, and steel greys. No reds or yellows. Sound and smell were similarly diminished, and strange things were starting to happen: queer sightings and peculiar noises, as if our sense-starved brains, accustomed as they were to processing vast amounts of information on land, were compensating by filling in the gaps, *creating* things that weren't really there.

A week before, for instance, I'd seen the wizened expression of a white-bearded man in the face of a breaking wave. Rational cognizance caught up a fraction of a second later, and made the editorial correction to what it really was: just a pattern made by white foam. Something similar happened the next day when the smell of bacon and eggs was so real I began salivating. The source revealed itself as a canvas compartment cover singed by the lighted stove. That same night the unnerving sound of a child shrieking in the darkness turned out to be the wind howling through the aluminium fins of the radar reflector.

The common link was mistaken identity, the brain attaching the wrong label to interpret the world around us. In the case of the old man, raw sense data travelled as electrochemical impulses from the eye to the optical centre which, being slower than usual through underuse, temporarily assigned the wrong image. The mistake was quickly detected, a hasty edit made, and the correct version of reality made available to consciousness.

This theory led us to speculate about mermaids. Sailors on long sea voyages in the Golden Age of Sail would have been subjected to the same mental atrophy as we were. A homesick crewman might have seen a familiar pattern in the water, reminding him of a sorely missed sweetheart. Before the mind had time to make the correction, he would have yelled out the dramatic sighting. Seeing nothing but water, his friends would have turned on the poor deluded soul, who now faced looking like a complete fool. Better to stick to the original story, even embellish it a little, adding she disappeared so quickly because of her fish-like tail, instead of having to admit to going soft in the head.

THE HONEYMOON DIDN'T last. Another contretemps had us back at each other's throats a few days later, this time over a proposal by Steve to make a detour via the British Virgin Islands. Two of his friends, Tanya and Tubes, owned a water sports business there. The idea was to stop off before arriving in the US and alert the media. "Otherwise we'll roll up in Miami," Steve argued, "and no one will even know."

He had a point. Media coverage was key to leveraging the sponsorship we needed to keep the expedition afloat. But after weighing the pros and cons, I figured it wasn't worth it. The BVIs were 250 miles to the south, forfeiting the northerly advantage we'd worked so hard to maintain. If we couldn't regain our latitude, we'd miss the US altogether and be forced to set a course for Central America.* We wouldn't last long in countries like Honduras or Guatemala without any money. As poor as the local people were, we couldn't expect to fundraise, and the expedition would founder.

Besides, I smelt a rat. Being considerably closer than Miami, I was convinced the BVIs offered Steve an excuse to get off the boat sooner rather than later. He'd already voiced how much he was starting to resent life aboard, likening it to an exchange visit to France he'd endured as a fourteen-year-old. Alienated, homesick, and desperately unhappy, he'd withdrawn into his shell, numb to it all.

"My vote is to stay on course for Miami," I said firmly, going on to explain my concern about veering too far south. "The media coverage would be nice, but jeopardizing our chances of reaching North America is too great a risk, don't you agree?"

Steve didn't, and a protracted argument broke out instead.

Next morning, I was heating our porridge when something caught my eye. The chart stashed in the port side netting had been altered during the night, a faint line drawn in pencil connecting our position with

---

* Several experienced sailors had predicted we would end up in Barbados, 300 miles further south than the BVIs.

the BVIs. *Is this just a coincidence,* I wondered? Steve had altered course from 310 and was now pedalling 280 degrees. "Because we're not being taken south at the moment," he explained. His mood had rallied, and his revolutions per minute, usually around forty-two, were now above fifty. Was this also just coincidence?

I stopped stirring. "So, I have a question. Would you *like* to stop off at Tanya and Tubes?"

"Very much so!" Steve replied cheerfully. *A bit too cheerfully,* I thought. The evidence was incontrovertible: the change in heading, the increased RPM, the line on the chart, and now a confession. Anger boiled up inside me, constricting my throat and flushing my cheeks.

I stabbed a finger at him. "You're heading for the BVIs aren't you!"

Steve looked at me in dismay. "No! I wouldn't without first consulting you Jas—"

"Why the new heading then? Why the high spirits all of a sudden? Yesterday you said the only reason to go there would be for sponsorship reasons. Now you're saying you'd *like* to go there. You've just contradicted yourself!"

"I only drew the line as... as... a theoretical marker," he stammered. "In case the conditions changed and we found ourselves being taken there anyway."

"What do you mean *being taken there anyway?* We could be taken to any one of a thousand islands in the Caribbean. Just admit it, you've already made the decision to go whether I like it or not!"

Steve opened his mouth to defend himself, but I was on a roll. "Right!" I yelled. "That's it. There's no fucking way I'm going to the BVIs now!"

We glared at each other, both itching to launch in and start pummelling. Without breaking my gaze, I finished my porridge, hacking at it with short stabs and jamming the stuff in my mouth. Steve continued to pedal, fists clenched, empty plate poised in his hand like a Japanese throwing star.

Fixing me with his piercing stare, he flexed his jaw, and said, "I don't believe you would have agreed to the idea for *any* reason, Jason." He raised his chin a fraction. "You're only hostile to it because it was *my* idea."

"Bullshit!"

The gloves were off again, and a fortnight of suppressed resentments sallied forth, the unaired grievances launched back and forth in angry salvoes.

It was Steve who pulled us back from the brink. "Listen, Jason, I give you my *word* I never wanted to go to the BVIs just to get to land."

What could anyone say to that? I had to accept it, of course. But dark thoughts continued to flail in my head like debris caught in a tornado. The fact was, I didn't know what to believe anymore.

"I have to call into question," he added a little later, "your reasons for wanting to stay north. It doesn't bode well for the remainder of the expedition."

Doesn't bode well for the remainder of the expedition? I mouthed the words. *Bloody cheek!*

"I'm going to… pretend I didn't hear that remark," I said, looking sideways into the sea, barely able to utter the words for suffocating fury.

NEXT DAY, TEMPER subdued, I resolved to step back and analyse the root cause of our dispute. Was it just natural competitiveness as I'd presumed cycling through Europe? Or did the confines of our living space compound aggression? Studies of laboratory rats show a link between cage size and behaviour. When living area is reduced below seventeen square inches per animal, hostility between cage-mates markedly increases.

There were undoubtedly other contributing factors. My wilderness immersion programme, by its very nature requiring self-absorption, was making me a poor companion and a bad team player. Steve was also having a tougher time adapting to life at sea than he'd anticipated. As we were only now finding out, the reality of being on an expedition—in particular crossing an ocean by human power—was little more than a day-to-day grind. There was nothing romantic in being cold, wet, and seasick. Only the passage of time and dimming of memory would imbibe these experiences with any sentimental, quixotic appeal.

But there was something else.

Steve's leadership style reminded me of the four months I'd spent at an army boot camp in Yorkshire. I'd hated taking orders as a nineteen-year-old, and I hated taking orders now. The aversion stemmed from early childhood. My father was a faultless provider for the family, and as his son I never once doubted his love for me. But the combination of his commanding presence as a career officer in the Royal Tank Regiment and my innate hostility towards authority ran together like oil and water.

Poor old Steve didn't know it, but he'd unwittingly become my surrogate father, and I unwittingly resented him for it.

He was right about one thing. The Atlantic voyage was a test case for the remainder of the expedition, and deteriorating trust between us didn't augur well. Unless I could better integrate my philosophical inquiry, and Steve reconcile himself with life aboard, we were in deep trouble for the Pacific, three times the distance of the Atlantic.

As IF SENSING the atmosphere of disgruntlement, the gearbox, whose function was to transfer drive from the pedal system through ninety degrees to the propeller shaft, began an intermittent, high-pitched whine. Originally designed for high-speed industrial applications, we'd been assured the unit could more than handle our low RPMs. But somehow the hub had worked loose, breaking the seal and allowing precious fluid to escape. The bearings wouldn't last long without lubrication, and being a sealed unit, there was no way to replace them.

Steve suggested drilling a hole through the top of the casing to allow a grease point to be fitted. I was unconvinced. Without a spare, we had one shot at getting it right. What if we botched the drilling and put the internal gearing out of whack? We'd be forced to use the oars, the doomsday scenario to avoid at all costs...

"I reckon we drill only if the noise gets worse," I said.

Steve stared at me in disbelief. His expression said it all: *You've just torpedoed another of my ideas, just because it's my idea...*

Had I? It was difficult to be objective anymore, keeping crucial decisions such as this free of emotional bias.

Later, when Steve was asleep, I experimented using a non-invasive method of getting lubricant to the bearings: pouring olive oil down a length of cotton thread from the sewing kit, through the tiny gap created by the broken seal. I'd let a few drops through, turn the pedals, repeat the process, and so on. Olive oil wasn't the lubricant of choice, but sunscreen was the only other option. The squealing grew quieter. Then stopped altogether. But for how long?

Christmas Eve, 1994

IT WAS WHILE listening to the King's College Cambridge carol service, dulcet harmonies wending their way to us courtesy of the BBC World Service airwaves, that we began to feel homesick. Back home, our families would be sitting around log fires, roasting chestnuts. Christmas trees would be dripping with tinsel and lights, gaily coloured presents strewn underneath. *The Wizard of Oz* would be playing on the box. Would our folks be missing us as much as we were them? Of course. Not for the first time since leaving Lagos, Steve and I looked at each other with the same thought.

What the hell are we doing here?

It was my turn for a longer stint in the Rathole. Before sliding in, I glanced through the forward window. An odd pattern of lights was bobbing on the horizon.

"There's a ship to the southwest," I said.

Steve was taking a break from pedalling, his arms crossed, legs at rest. "I've been watching it for a while. Doesn't seem to be moving. Those lights don't look familiar, either."

He reached for the laminated navigation card stashed in the netting above his head.

"Red over white over red means *vessel restricted in its ability to manoeuvre.* I'll keep an eye on it. You get some sleep, Jase."

I was out cold by the time my head touched the pillow, already dreaming of the mouth-watering Christmas dinner we had planned for the next day: stale mutton granules reconstituted with water and mashed potato powder.

AT DAWN, THE ship was still there, only closer, and displaying the day-time version of the same set of lights: a black ball hanging over a black diamond over a black ball.

Steve looked groggy. After pedalling until three in the morning, he'd curled up on the bottom of the boat and tried to grab a few hours of sleep, legs and arms wrapped around the pedal unit. It had rained during the night, adding to his misery. We mumbled Merry Christmas to each other, and then switched. It was December 25, 1994, day sixty-nine of the voyage.

With my mother's Christmas cake already gone, the day would be no different to any other. For a while we'd managed to keep alive a glimmer of seasonal cheer with the prospect of finding two *Mrs Peek's Christmas Puddings* buried under the canvas bunk. That is until they were finally unearthed, looking flatter than piss on a plate after being slept on for two and a half months.

We ate breakfast, the same instant oats we had every morning, and sat gazing absentmindedly at the mystery ship, now only a mile and a half to the southeast. The inscription *AT&T* was stamped on one of its enormous white funnels. American. Had they stopped to celebrate Christmas?

Until now, we hadn't felt like making contact with other ships. A bulk ore carrier had passed a week previously, an ugly-looking thing streaked with rust, columns of black soot belching from its smokestacks. We hadn't even switched the radio on. Intimidated by the thought of any foreign object entering our private little universe, life on Planet *Moksha* had become entirely insular.

But this was different. It was Christmas. There was a stationary ship within spitting distance. It was American more to the point, stuffed to the gunwales with all manner of goodies no doubt. What more did we want? For a red bow to be tied around it, and uniformed waiters to walk across the water and serve us Christmas dinner on a silver platter?

Steve and I looked at each other and grinned, the same *"I dare you!"* grin that once led to the pink cock and hairy balls incident.

The VHF radio suddenly burst to life, startling us with an 'All Stations Advisory'. A cable laying ship was repairing submarine tele-communications cables in the area. *"All other vessels to remain clear,"* the voice barked.

It had to be them.

Steve unclipped the handheld microphone and spoke with clipped formality. "USCS Charles L. Brown"—he was repeating the vessel's name—"this is pedal boat *Moksha, Moksha*. Over."

Nothing.

On the third attempt, a laconic drawl, thin on radio etiquette, asked for identification.

"USCS Charles L. Brown," Steve replied, "We are a British registered, twenty-six-foot human-powered boat en route to Miami, at sea for sixty-nine days now. Our only means of propulsion is pedal power. Over."

The voice came back, this time sounding agitated.

"Is this George down in the engine room again? Knock it off big guy. Channel sixteen ain't the place for stoopid Christmas jokes. Anyway, your Limey accent sucks."

Steve tried again. "Captain, look out over your starboard beam and you'll see us."

There was silence for several seconds. Then, "Err.... roger that... *Mucksow*. How can we help?"

Half an hour later, we were scrambling up a rope ladder swinging against a thirty-foot wall of steel, *"Mucksow"* secured against two enormous fenders lowered down by the deckhands.

Steve's deliberately open to interpretation "we'd love to share a little Christmas cheer with you guys" had worked a treat. The skipper, Captain Dooley, had given us permission to come aboard while his engineers finished splicing the underwater telecommunications cable between Europe and North America.

At the top of the ladder, we swung our legs over the rail, and for the first time since Madeira tried to walk. Several crewmembers in red and blue coveralls gathered to watch. When I stepped forward with my right foot, it spun the half circle of a pedal stroke. My left foot tried to complete the rotation, sending me to my knees.

"We've got the strongest legs here," Steve laughed, "and we need walking frames!"

I tried again, this time managing to stagger three paces before the urge to pedal kicked in. Walking felt so bloody weird! Dishevelled, wearing only rags, coated in salt and peppered with saltwater boils, we must have looked like a pair of paralytic pirates with bubonic plague.

A man wearing a white jump suit stepped forward and introduced himself as the First Officer. "But just call me Ken," he added, waving a hand dismissively.

Middle aged with a cannonball head and fatherly expression, Ken said he'd been at sea all his life. "Thought I'd seen everything," he chuckled hoarsely, "'til you guys turned up. What in God's name got into your heads to want to pedal across the Atlantic?"

It was an excellent question. While Steve did his best to answer it, Ken led us to a mess room where a linen-covered table groaned under an orgy of sensory delights. Baskets of freshly baked bread. Refrigerated squares of butter. A bottle of Chateauneuf du Pape Blanc 1990. And the magnum opus: two plates piled high with turkey breast, Brussels sprouts, roast potatoes, and stuffing, all lathered in thick layers of steaming gravy.

Steve almost burst into tears.

"I've had second thoughts," I said, pushing my plate away. "I don't want to spoil my appetite for the mutton granules. You can have mine if you like."

Looking at me like I'd lost my mind, Steve reached over and stabbed a slice of turkey with his fork.

"Not!" I cried, smacking his hand away.

The temptation to do away with utensils altogether and revert to caveman etiquette, plunging face first into the heavenly mound of seasonal fodder, was overwhelming. We had company, though.

Two deckhands, Robin and Larry, were sitting opposite, interrogating us about the voyage. Answering their questions revealed a multitasking nightmare: eating and talking at the same time. Both functions relied on the same orifice, creating a bottleneck of incoming food and outgoing words. The two met in the middle, wrestling each other in a garbled mish-mash of half eaten vocabulary and tongue-tied bits of chow.

Yet, in spite of the oral handicap, we giddily inhaled the extremes of textures and flavours, and the food evaporated. As we were scraping the last morsels from our plates and stuffing the remaining bread rolls into our pockets, Ken returned from the bridge.

"Would you guys like a hot shower?"

Those first seconds of hot water splashing over my face were euphoric, mouth agape in orgiastic bliss, salt sloughing off my skin like a snake shedding its leathery hide. And the indulgence didn't stop there. After we'd rubbed down with towels bigger than Australia and softer than slumber, Santa Ken had one more surprise in store.

"Cap'n wants to extend each of you a gift from *AT&T.* A call home."
Wow! Was this the Good Ship Lollipop, or what!

Up in the control room, the communications officer connected us each in turn. Madeira was the last time our families had confirmation we were both alive and well. What would they make of receiving a call from the middle of the Atlantic?

The comparatively recent advent of satellite communications proved a hurdle between my mother and I, however.

"Hello... Ma? Happy Christmas!"

"Who is this?"

"Jason."

"*Who?*"

"Jason—your son." *Maybe my voice sounds different with the compression?*

"That's impossible," she said flatly. "He's in the middle of the Atlantic."

"Exactly! We're on an American cable laying ship, and they've kindly let us use their satellite phone."

Pause. I could hear my mother muttering to my father in the background, something about one of Jason's dreadful friends and a practical joke.

"Mother, it's me!"

Finally, the penny dropped. She began peeping with excitement. "Oh, oh, oh, oh!"

After we were done, word arrived from the bridge that the fibre optic cable had been fixed, and the ship was ready to get underway. Everyone else in the Western world could now bid their transatlantic friends and families season's greetings. Our Alice in Wonderland experience was at an end.

Thanking our Yuletide hosts for their gracious hospitality, Steve and I climbed back down the rope ladder to where *Moksha* surged in the swell, and prepared to cast off.

"Psssst! Hey guys..."

It was George, the rogue engineer-cum-prankster, leaning out of one of the portholes. In his hands was a brown parcel secured with string.

"Figured you could do with a little light reading out there," he said with a wink.

The package came sailing through the air and landed with a resounding thud in the bottom of the boat.

Opening it later, we found nothing of particular interest. Just the latest edition of the Economist, a week old copy of the Miami Herald, and, at the bottom, a large stack of porn.

MY DIRTY WORDS campaign inevitably arrived at truth. Was it like the word for understanding, I wondered, with rational as well as intuitive meaning? If so, was the rational version the same as Thoreau's truth, the ultimate truth I'd been searching for?

The Oxford Dictionary would have me believe so, defining truth *'that which is... in accordance with fact or reality'*. In other words, truth was something fixed and unchanging, independent of the subjective whims of human consciousness, proven to exist only through scientific observation—like a dog being a warm blooded, carnivorous animal, equipped with a fur coat and tail, walking on all fours. Such characteristics were immutable, their "realness" proved beyond all rational doubt by measuring heart rate, body temperature, food intake, and other manifest criteria.

Yet, one of science's founding fathers once declared, "The supreme task [of the physicist] is to arrive at those universal elementary laws from which the cosmos can be built up by pure deduction. There is no logical path to these laws; *only intuition, resting on sympathetic understanding of experience,* can reach them."

According to Albert Einstein, who wasn't alone in his belief, hard scientific facts and their associated truths, rather than being at odds with subjective experience, were actually *created* by it (or discovered, depending on which school of thought you subscribed to).* Institutionalized science, on the other hand, maintained that the laws underpinning reality only became truth after being observed through a microscope.

So, who was right?

Ultimate truth existed, but the source of it was in dispute. Maybe it was a problem of labelling, similar to when I'd mistaken a flip-flop for a scorpion fish a few days earlier. The fish had *seemed* real enough, at least for a fraction of a second. But by morphing into a flip-flop, it showed how reality is just an arbitrary label created in the visual cortex, the brain's interpretation of electrochemical impulses streaming along the

---

* The early twentieth century English author Gilbert Chesterton once declared, "You can only find truth with logic if you have already found truth without it." Similarly, the nineteenth century French mathematician, Henri Poincaré, admitted that more often than not he *felt* the solutions to mathematical problems through the pre-intellectual subliminal self before the rational side kicked in. For this, he argued, a catalyst, like a seed crystal, was first needed to trigger such episodes of intuitive thought expansion, ultimately leading to empirical understanding of phenomena.

optic nerve. In that sense, the "I" creates the world around us.

Similarly, Einstein's formula for E=mc^2 was merely a label he invented to represent the various phenomena associated with his theory of relativity. Mathematical symbols were the purest way to share his subjective revelations with the outside world, translating them to objective scientific truths in the process.

Could this be the source of the confusion? Words, images, symbols, and formulas were agents of truth, not ultimate truth itself. They were mechanisms to share the probability of phenomena behaving in a certain way, thus becoming laws, but subordinate nonetheless to a deeper layer of understanding that only subjective, intuitive experience could reach. Over the centuries, the two truths had merged and were now indistinguishable, the external packaging as if not more important than the underlying form it represented.

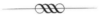

January 15

DAY NINETY OF the voyage meant two things: we'd been at sea for a quarter of a year, and we were down to a fortnight's worth of rations. Calculating the total crossing couldn't possibly take more than three months, I'd provisioned the boat for 106 days at sea, a figure that included a twenty per cent contingency. Now we would need every scrap of food just to reach the Bahamas, still over a thousand miles away.

We debated whether or not to go to half rations. My reason for doing so, even if it meant our emaciated bodies started burning muscle, was to remain alive after day 106. Steve wasn't keen on the idea. His thinking was the same that led us to devour the Christmas cake early. To keep as strong as we could, as long as we could, and hope some other means of resupply presented itself before day 107.

One obvious thing was to start fishing more. *Moksha* was a mobile sushi bar with all the dorado milling around, using her as a base from which to launch forays against the schools of flying fish startled into the air by our lumbering approach. Even with our miserable fishing record, we hoped to catch at least a few of them, the largest of which we'd pre-emptively named 107.

The flying fish themselves were already contributing to the pot—albeit through no skill of our own. Most mornings we'd find a handful of them knocked unconscious in the gunwales. "The unluckiest fish in the Atlantic," Steve called them, a reference to being unfortunate enough to collide with the only solid object in hundreds of thousands of square miles of otherwise unimpeded ocean. During the graveyard shifts, a thud against the cabin would alert us to another fatal collision. At daybreak there they would be, staring up at us with lifeless, goggling eyes, ready to be scooped up and tossed in the frying pan for breakfast.

By day, these same fishes regaled us with spectacular feats of acrobatic comedy, flouting the jaws of our marauding dorado flotilla. A few energetic flicks of their propeller-like tails, and whole troupes of them would break the surface, shimmying over the water like cartoon characters tap dancing across a liquid stage. Once enough speed was gained for their fins to take over as wings—Lift Off! The air would fill with little silver torpedoes, the snapping dorados bounding in their wake.

Another consequence of diminishing supplies was the boat becoming increasingly tippy. *Moksha's* ability to self-right depended on the stores acting as ballast. We should have thought to bring along collapsible containers to fill with seawater and replace the lost weight as we went. But hindsight is always twenty-twenty, and such unpreparedness only served to remind us how isolated we were, and how popping out to the hardware store was only a distant memory.

Two days earlier, we'd been hit by another storm. The wind had driven us back thirty-two miles before veering around the compass and allowing us to make headway again. For the next 48 hours, the waves remained huge. Every time one of them muscled up astern, *Moksha* wobbled unnervingly, jostled by the energy massed in the barging crest.

Steering in these conditions demanded every ounce of concentration. Being long and narrow, *Moksha* cut down the face of a wave like a surfboard. The pedaller could estimate the size of the wave by the tilt of the bow, and the degree to which the pedal system tightened with the force of water sucking backwards. The cranks would recoil like a spring—*tighter…tighter…tighter*—until all hell broke loose in an explosion of furiously spinning pedals and spitting foam as the boat hurtled forward with gut-wrenching acceleration. Effective helmsmanship at this point amounted to hanging on for dear life to the two steering toggles, thrusting them forward and back in a desperate bid to keep *Moksha* heading perpendicular. Slewing to port or starboard could be disastrous, leading to a broach, or even capsize.

Personally, I found this invigorating. The adrenaline rush of operating the boat on such a knife-edge was the perfect antidote to Creeping Grey Funk. And keeping the hatch open and the air circulating prevented the inside of the boat from turning into a sauna.

Steve didn't care for it, though, especially not the open-air approach. He preferred to keep the hatch more closed than open in case of capsize. As he reminded me, if all three inner compartments flooded, *Moksha* would sink, and probably quicker than either of the one-person life rafts could be deployed.

Our disagreement deteriorated into a childish tussle of push-me-pull-you. I would slide the hatch open at the beginning of my shift. Steve would close it at the beginning of his.

I should have been more respectful of my partner's comfort zone, but at the time I didn't give a damn. Following the row over the BVIs, anger had resurfaced about other injustices, including Steve's disregard for my comfort zone and presumed complicity in how the boat builders were treated. That he was proving to be a bit of a girl's blouse hacking it on the expedition he'd pushed and bullied to get going in the first place only heightened the sense of comeuppance.

Secretly, I drew pleasure in being the stronger psychologically as well as physically: pumping more water, and vacating the Rathole quicker when it was my turn to pedal. But as the voyage wore on, I saw how such competitiveness yields only false power. Like a canker, it grew as self-disgust, eventually turning to guilt, that in spite of being the stronger pedaller with more self-discipline, I hadn't been strong enough to rise above my resentments and be a better friend.

By 3:00 pm, the wave height had increased to twenty-five feet. Before taking over, I clambered out onto the foredeck with my stills camera to capture some of the more dramatic waves crashing over the stern. Being a manual, I needed both hands to operate the shutter and focus ring. This meant having to grip the front compartment with my lower legs and ride *Moksha* hands-free like a bronco. It was stupidly dangerous. But in those days, I was dangerously stupid.

"Wahoooo! What a rush!" I hooted, jumping back into the cockpit and slamming the hatch shut as another deluge of water thundered past. "Got some great shots, too!"

Steve replied with a quick nod, his face steeled in concentration working the steering lines. He looked frazzled.

Switching positions had to be done as quickly as possible. Once settled in the pedal seat, I grabbed The Pixies' *Doolittle* from the sealed box containing our cassettes, slid it into the Walkman, and got to work. Steve, meanwhile, retrieved the desalinator pump from the grab bag, and began lashing it to one of the emergency oars.*Down to just half a litre of drinking water, we desperately needed to replenish.

I'd heard about Rogue Waves, walls of water recorded as high as

---

* The grab bag was the most important thing to bail into the life rafts with. It was filled with essential survival equipment: EPIRB, compass, mirrors for signalling aircraft, bags of water, and a few days of food.

one hundred feet, and preceded by troughs deep enough to be termed "holes in the sea." To the mariner these were the most feared waves of all, the tsunamis of deep water, vast, pulverizing mountains of raw energy careering along the ocean highways, levelling all in their path. The crests alone were enough to pitchpole a boat, somersaulting the stern over the bow.

One of these monsters was now barrelling up astern, announcing its imminent arrival with a terrifying hiss. *Moksha* suddenly dropped fifteen feet into the hole, and her stern thrust violently skyward. I found myself gaping down a forty-foot precipice, certain we were going over. A dreadful freeze-frame moment, long enough for my heart to leap into my mouth, and then we were in free fall.

Steering gone, we hurtled downwards, surf thundering all around. *Moksha's* nose lifted a fraction off the vertical. Instead of pitchpoling, the stern overtook the bow in a slow, almost elegant broach to starboard.

Our world turned upside down.

All was confusion. Water planed through the open hatch, roiling in my eyes and ears, forcing my head and torso back against the pedal seat. Even capsized we were going more than ten knots.

Seconds later, another gut-wrenching spin, and streaks of brilliant sky appeared where the bottom of the boat had been. *Moksha* had self-righted. The central compartment was swamped, though. I sat stunned by the chaos before me: sodden charts, submerged packets of food, pots and pans clanking to and fro, the sea anchor rope hopelessly tangled around the pedal unit. It was a disaster area of gear on the move. The cassette container, now waterlogged, bobbed around my knees. Gabriel Garcia Marquez's *One Hundred Years of Solitude* drifted past.

The boat looked structurally intact. Even vital equipment like the compass and radio appeared unharmed. There was, however, one important thing missing.

Steve.

One minute he'd been standing there, pumping water. The next he was gone.

"C'mon Steve," I chuckled. "Stop pissing about. Where are you hiding?"

I scrambled forward, sloshing through the debris, tripping over the headphone cord mid-cabin. Recovering myself, I peered into the Rathole. Had he managed to dive in there at the last second?

It was empty.

The laughter dried in my throat as I began processing the full significance of what had happened. *If he's not inside the boat, he must have gone overboard... And he wasn't wearing a safety harness...*

I thrust my head clear of the hatch, frantically scouring the surrounding ocean. All I needed was a head, an arm—anything. Then I could either throw a line if he was close enough, or try to keep *Moksha* from drifting until he swam to safety. It was pointless trying to make a U-turn in these seas. With only a third of a horsepower at my disposal, all I would achieve was to travel parallel to the waves, away from the spot he'd gone overboard.

But there was nothing. No sign of life between the towering peaks. As the seconds passed, I imagined him knocked unconscious and already drowned.

Horror and guilt swooped into my stomach. What would I tell his family when I showed up alone in Miami? Surely they'd suspect me of throwing him overboard after all the fights we'd had.

Hang on. You're getting paranoid. Only you and Steve know about those...

Yes, but if I'd closed the hatch like he asked, he might still be alive. How will I ever live with the guilt?

Fuck the guilt. Let's face it. The bastard deserved it...

That's not true! Another minute out on the deck taking photos and *I* would be the one out there now. It should have happened to me.

Whatever. The secret will die with him, and no one will ever know…

A strange sound interrupted my mortifications, something bumping against the hull. Looking down the length of the boat, I saw an object the size and shape of a small mooring buoy bobbing next to the rudder.

Is that… Is that what I think it is?

The longer I stared at it, the more it took the form of a human head. For months I'd been looking at that ugly bloody thing. Now it was the most beautiful thing I'd ever seen.

"Steve!" I shouted jubilantly.

A claw-like hand hooked itself over the starboard gunwale. Then a death mask, eyes wide with terror, slowly turned to face me.

BACK IN THE cabin, wrapped in a towel and shivering uncontrollably, Steve recalled what had happened.

"It was like going over a waterfall." His eyes were shut tight, and his hands whirled around his head to emphasize the disorientation. "Total confusion. Not knowing which way was up or down."

He paused for a moment to gulp some tea. "Then my foot got snagged on something. It was pulling me underwater, faster and faster. I thought, this is it Stevie, you're done for—"

"I thought we were both done for," I cut in. "Fancy leaving me to pedal the rest of the way to Miami myself you selfish bugger!"

His mouth twitched at my lame attempt at humour. The truth was, he'd been incredibly lucky. A trailing line had saved him, miraculously wrapping itself around his ankle, keeping him tethered long enough to grab a hold. Otherwise, he would still be out there, swimming for his life, *Moksha* growing smaller and smaller until his arms couldn't sustain him any longer.

By January 22, we were nearing Mayaguana, the first in a six-hundred-mile chain of islands stretching all the way to Miami. Despite being the largest and most likely to support human settlement, the nub of land was marked as uninhabited on our chart. With resupply unlikely, Steve agreed to go to half rations. Our nine remaining days of food would have to stretch to three or more weeks. We also had two tots of whiskey, a pair of edible candles from the RAF life rafts, and half a tube of toothpaste, looking more and more appealing by the day.

We speculated which would give out first, the food or the gearbox. The latter had suffered a major grinding fit during my last graveyard shift. Olive oil had ceased to be effective, and the steel bearings were now grinding themselves to pieces. Every mile they held out was a glorious mile we didn't have to row.

It was also excruciatingly hot. During daylight hours, the pedaller was trapped in a suffocating cul-de-sac of spent air. Nights offered little relief. At one time the most prized real estate on the entire boat, the Rathole was now a sweltering oven, making it virtually impossible to sleep. Fatigue once again reared its ugly head.

Ironically, it was hot tea that kept us going. The celebrated coolant of colonial Brits wilting in the debilitating heat of tropical climes had become ours too. At 5:45 pm, I filled the kettle while Steve pedalled, his dripping torso crisscrossed like the tributaries of some great river delta. His face bore a medley of extremes: chronic exhaustion, pain from the salt sores, and an air of fed-up-ness at the voyage in general. A ginger beard the size of a rhododendron bush swung from his gaping jaw. And once so intense, his eyes were dull and glassy, sunk back into their sockets. His legs worked in stiff, robotic thrusts against the gearbox that grated and squealed in defiance. *A man at the end of his tether...* I scribbled in my journal. Yet here he was, soldiering on, the epitome of indomitable grit in the face of so much hardship.

A white parrot hove into view, a beautiful thing with long ivory tail feathers, making laborious progress against the wind. Aside from a rocket fired from Cape Canaveral earlier in the day, the bird was the first evidence of land we'd seen. *Where does it think it's going?* I wondered. There was nothing out east apart from open water, certainly nowhere to land. *Maybe it's gone a bit funny in the head. Happens out here…*

A series of beeps announced the six o'clock news on the BBC World Service. The Mexican Army was accused of human rights abuses cleaning up Zapatista rebels in Chiapas. Twenty-two cases of maritime piracy had been reported in Indonesian waters between 1994 and 1995. Both, I remarked to Steve, sounded like hellholes we should try to avoid. Then, more violence, more suffering, more greed…

"Isn't there anything else?" Steve said irritably. "I can't handle all this depressing shite!"

The rest of the dial offered little better: Christian evangelists hawking their trade to lost souls; drying-out clinics soliciting alcoholics and junkies; health farms targeting the overweight. America, in all her glory, beckoned.

I flicked back to the BBC. My old indie pop idol, John Peel, was on now, playing his usual mishmash of alternative releases. *Boy, does that old dog have a piss-easy life*, I thought. *Wandering into Bush House once a week, throwing on a handful of records he's found under his bed, then wandering out half an hour later with 500 quid in his pocket. Money for old rope…*

He had a great delivery, though, saying the first pea-brained thing that came into his head. "This track makes me think of a man walking in the snow and ice, calling out his friend's name…"

Zzzzzmmmmmmzzzmmmm…

What's that? Static on the radio perhaps.

I twiddled the dial.

Vvrrrrrrzzzzzmmmmmmmm…

Getting louder, like an engine.

Steve and I snapped from our reveries. The ship must be almost upon us!

But there was nothing, only the deep sapphire of the sea rolling out to the horizon.

"It's a plane!" Steve cried. Seconds later, a Cessna roared overhead, lone hand waving from the starboard window. "Who the he—"

"It's that bloody Scotsman," I chortled. "I wonder who he nicked the plane from?"

Somehow, I always knew Our Man Brown would find us. Steve had phoned him from the USCS Charles L. Brown to report another problem with our video camera. Already gaining a reputation for his daredevil camerawork and ability to jerry-rig miracles out of moonshine, the MacGyver-like Scot had responded by saying he'd "find a way hook or by crook" to get us a second camera before Miami. Such an assurance from anyone else could be forgiven as fanciful good intention. But this was Kenny, Scotland's answer to the Swiss Army knife. The job was as good as done.

Later, we learned how he'd had quite an ordeal getting to the Caribbean himself, working construction in New York City to pay for his flight from London, hitchhiking a thousand miles to Miami, then wangling free passage to the island of Providenciales in the Turks and Caicos. Upon arrival he'd befriended the resident GP, Doctor Sam Flattery, who knew the owner of the only light aircraft on the island. For hours they'd flown a grid, scouring the ocean from horizon to horizon. *Moksha* being the same colour as the innumerable white caps hadn't helped. Just as the fuel warning light started blinking, Doctor Sam caught a reflection off one of *Moksha's* tinted windows.

"*Moksha, Moksha*," the radio barked, "Kenny here, over."

Steve switched on the VHF and handed me the mouthpiece.

"I never thought I'd be so glad to hear a Scotsman's voice," I replied. "Over!"

With their fuel running low, an immediate decision had to be made. Either we carried on to Miami, and hoped some hastily prepared snacks dropped with the replacement video camera would get us there. Or we stopped in at Providenciales, just thirty-three miles to the southwest, got properly resupplied and the gearbox repaired, then continued.

"Oh aye, and not that this'll make any difference," Kenny added, "but Providenciales is full ay nice folk, great food, and *cold beer*…"

It was a no-brainer. We immediately set a course for Turtle Cove Marina on the north shore of the island.

Before turning for home, Kenny came through one last time on the radio. "Might as well fling ye doon these goodies. Give ye somethin' tae munch oan tonight."

The plane banked sharply and made a final pass. A dark shape appeared out of the passenger window, plummeting towards *Moksha* like a homing missile.

"Take cover!" I yelled.

The projectile cannoned into the water just off our starboard beam.

"Jesus," Steve breathed. "That was close!"

A few feet to the left, and we would have suffered the supreme ignominy of being scuttled by our cameraman. I could imagine what *The Daily Star* would have to say about that.

PEDAL SUB SUNK. AGAIN!

After 97 days at sea, a pedal-powered submarine used by two young Britons to cross the Atlantic was today sunk by their own airdrop. The deadly package contained half a pound of cheese, three oranges, a loaf of bread, and two cans of Miller Light beer.

7:51 am. Day 98

NUDGED BY A light breeze, *Moksha* drifted gently towards a ribbon of white sand capped by low-lying greenery. It was early still, but the sun already felt uncomfortably hot against our skin.

Compared to the ninety-seven preceding nights, pedalling through the darkness had been a piece of cake assisted by our new and exciting range of psychological carrots. The plastic cheese and white bread were my favourites; the fresh oranges tasted bitter after our sugar-laden diet, and the beer as disgusting as I remembered it aged nine, sneaking a sip from my dad's pint in The Oxenham Arms. Even more beguiling were the abundance of sensory delights just over the horizon: a non-moving bed, cold drinks, hot water, phones, laughter, and long conversations (well, just conversations). We completed the distance in record time, arriving at our rendezvous point two hours ahead of schedule.

At 8:00 am, we hailed Kenny on the VHF to arrange a pilot to guide us through the reef. Our tartan cousin sounded groggy and hungover, muttering something about a cat shiteing in his mouth during the night.

"We'll be oot in aboot an 'oor," he grunted.

Steve was transformed, gobbling his breakfast, and racing to reposition the pedal seat at the end of each shift. The mirage that had kept him going for so many hours, days, and months was now so close he could almost reach out and touch it. Land, at last!

I, on the other hand, felt somewhat ambivalent. Kenny and Doctor Sam rolling up had been thrilling at first, before the repercussions of making landfall sooner than expected began sinking in. My wilderness immersion programme was starting to bear fruit, revealing encouraging glimpses into the workings of consciousness, in particular language, cognition, and sense of self. But there were still so many unanswered questions, including the most important, the core of ultimate truth. Back on land, surrounded by humanity's myriad distractions, resolution would be all but impossible.

At least I'd achieved one of my main objectives: to feel as reluctant to leave this world of shifting blue as I was to leave the solid one of green all those months ago.

THE CARIBBEAN
REEFS, PIRATES, & MAGGOTY SALT SORES

What was the meaning of that South-Sea Exploring Expedition, with all its parade and expense, but an indirect recognition of the fact that there are continents and seas in the moral world to which every man is an isthmus or an inlet, yet unexplored by him, but that it is easier to sail many thousands of miles through cold and storm and cannibals, in a government ship, with five hundred men and boys to assist one, than it is to explore the private sea, the Atlantic and Pacific Ocean of one's being alone.

—HENRY DAVID THOREAU, *Walden*

KENNY ARRIVED IN AN off-white motorboat driven by Darren, a congenial if spaced-out-looking teenager from the Provo Turtle Divers Centre.

"Hey! *Bearrrdy!*" hollered Kenny at the sight of Steve. He had his camera levelled on his shoulder in the exact same pose we'd last seen him off the coast of Portugal. "Got the full-on explorer look!"

Rafting up, we discussed the plan for crossing the reef. Being low tide, we would have to navigate one of the narrow fifty-foot cuts between the serrated jaws of coral.

Darren and Kenny took the lead, *Moksha* following in their wake. As I pedalled, the launch dipped in and out of sight behind the rolling waves. Suddenly, it disappeared altogether.

"Shit, they're in trouble!" yelled Steve, watching through a pair of binoculars. A curtain of surf exploded ahead of us, turning the reef into a deluge of white fury. The launch appeared a few seconds later, released like a champagne cork. "They've missed the cut, Jase. Turn around!"

But the reef was less than fifty paces away. We were going over whether we liked it or not. "Too late!" I cried, trying to pick up speed. If we turned beam-on, *Moksha* would be rolled and smashed against the razor-sharp coral heads. Steve reached forward and slammed the hatch shut as a pulse of water pushed *Moksha's* stern upwards. Her nose dropped. I could feel the water sucking backwards, the pedal system *tightening … tightening … tightening…*

"Hang on!"

Then the rollercoaster ride down the face of the wave…

KERRRRAAACCCCKKK!

The sound of splintering wood cut like canon fire through the bellowing surf.

"We've hit the reef!"

Seawater began spewing in through an eighteen-inch gash in the centreboard casing. Being the lowest part of the boat, the wooden keel had hit the reef first, punching it backwards and upwards, ripping through the hull like a can opener. Within seconds, water was up to our ankles. To assess the damage, Steve grabbed the foam cushion from the top of the centreboard and flung it aft. It landed squarely on the pedals.

"Get that fucking thing off there!" I screamed. The next wave was coiling up astern, getting ready to strike. *Moksha* was now lying parallel to the waves, jammed on the reef like a stuck pig. *This one will have us over*, I thought.

The leading edge of the next wave unstuck the centreboard in the same instant Steve snatched the cushion away. Flinging the rudder hard to port, I started pumping at the cranks to turn us off the horizontal.

Moksha responded with glacial slowness, moving degree by miserable degree back to our former right-angled position. *Twenty-five degrees… Thirty-five degrees… Forty-five degrees…*

The wave rumbled and the crest curled. The stern lifted in that all too familiar choreographed motion. Then water was slamming into the starboard quarter, rolling us to port and hurling our bodies against the inside of the cabin. *Moksha* corkscrewed in a gut-wrenching figure of eight on the tip of the wave's tongue. I braced for the imminent capsize…

It never came. We found ourselves instead slicing forward on a velveteen carpet of hissing foam, like a rollercoaster levelling out after the final hair-raising loop-the-loop. It was the earlier collision that had saved us, the fast-rising water giving *Moksha* more ballast than she'd had in a month.

USING THE BREADBOARD as a mallet, Steve managed to pound the centreboard back into alignment, stemming the gushing water to a manageable trickle. We then began our final approach, spangled sunlight dancing in the gentle chop of a turquoise lagoon, its crystalline water shimmering to a bleached sandy bottom. While Steve sat on the foredeck watching for submerged coral heads, I pedalled and tried to collect my thoughts. There was a danger of rushing the rainbow, of overindulging in all the things "missing" from our lives on *Moksha*. Deep down, I knew the diversions wouldn't last long. A few days of sense pleasure and any clarity of mind would cloud like a pool stirred with sediment.

These were the last breaths before the big plunge, a point of suspended animation before reality streaked off into uncharted waters like a struck dorado fish on the line, its freedom torn away. The brave new world of terra firma was now the unknown, a wild unpredictable thing as volatile and capricious as a raging bull. And all I could hope for was to hang onto its rucking flanks and try not to be thrown.

I've mastered self-control. I'm ready to resist all tempta—

"Yoo-hoo! Hey guys!"

Not fifty feet away was a bronzed, bikini-clad beauty waving from the beach. "Welcome to the Turks and Caicos!" she laughed, porcelain-white teeth flashing in the sun.

Well, I thought I was ready…

Island children blowing conch shells met us at the dockside. The British Overseas Territory of "Provo" welcomed us warmly and endearingly as their third most prestigious guests after Columbus—*"In fourteen hundred and ninety-two, Columbus sailed the ocean blue"*—and John Glenn, the first American returning from space in 1962.

"Did you get into any storms?" asked a young voice.

I should say! We rode thirty-five-foot waves from crest to trough! We capsized in towering seas! Both of us nearly drowned!

"Umm… Yes, we had some… some rough days," I replied awkwardly, swaying on the stationary jetty, then lapsed into silence. Bragging about the narrow escapes didn't appeal for some reason.

Wearing only rags, our first priority was to find some clothes before we were arrested for indecent exposure. I hit the local store with the entire expedition budget: a $50 note slipped into a copy of *Hustler* by the miscreant George.

Wandering like a lost child between the shelves, I found myself bombarded on all sides by strange shapes and exotic aromas, brightly painted tins, jars, and bottles. Everything was gently frying in a hot paste of extreme colour, the brilliant red and yellow containers of laundry detergent almost too garish to look at. I came to the bakery section. The aroma of fresh pastries had me salivating.

No, must resist temptation...

Minutes later, I walked out with four shopping bags filled with deliciously unhealthy crap: banana cakes, coconut cakes, jam rolls, and sweet bread. Half our money was gone, and we still didn't have any clothes.

So much for self-control...

The next day an invitation came through for *Moksha* to feature as a special exhibit in the 1995 Miami Boat Show. It was the perfect opportunity to start repaying the debt to Maria and our families by selling tee shirts and names on the boat. But with Miami still 550 miles away, and the show starting in a little over three weeks, the pressure was on to return to sea as quickly as possible.

Steve and Kenny immediately threw themselves into tasks: repairing the gearbox, re-provisioning the boat, sending out press releases, and arranging logistics for the boat show. Steve's fluid transition back to land mode was impressive, perhaps because he'd never really left it. I was useless by comparison. For the first 48 hours, all I could do was hole up in a complimentary hotel room with the curtains drawn. The four walls served as an improvised decompression chamber, allowing gradual acclimatization to the chaos raging beyond.

When, in due course, I did venture out, I wandered in a bubble, a thin but distinctive membrane separating me from my surroundings. It was fascinating if a little surreal observing "normal" life from the outside in, seeing how complicated our former lives once were. Even the languid island pace seemed turbocharged compared to the slow ocean plod. On land, time was a commodity that always seemed in short supply. I found myself yearning for deeper involvement, for genuine conversations with genuine people about genuine topics—topics with substance. Not just superficial chitchat skimming pebble-like across the surface of life. No sooner would I engage someone in discussion, than another person would appear, and the topic diluted. The bigger the group, the shallower social interaction became.

The nearest I got to one-on-one, focused dialogue was during a two-hour check-up with Doctor Sam, when he informed me that I'd lost fifteen per cent of my body weight. This wasn't the only deterioration, apparently.

"On an exhaustion scale of one to ten," he said, packing away his stethoscope, "With ten being pretty much unconscious, you and Steve were both at around eight and a half when you hit land."

And choice. Too much of it! For our fourth evening on Provo, we had three invitations: dinner at Jimmy's, drinks at the Banana Bar, or club night at Casablanca's. All I felt like doing, though, was sneaking down to the marina where *Moksha* was moored. There, under the cover of darkness, standing in the open hatch with a cup of hot chocolate in my hands, gazing up at the stars, I felt at peace.

By February 3, thanks mainly to the indefatigable efforts of Kenny, Steve and a small army of willing helpers, we were ready to make the final push to Miami. A friendly mechanic had succeeded in prying apart the gearbox and replacing the bearings. Provo Eats, a food importer, generously donated food. The icing on the cake was Doctor Sam pitching the owner of the American restaurant chain Arby's, who forked out $2,000 for a sticker on *Moksha's* hull for the big arrival. Steve had the bundle of notes in his hand for a full minute before Kenny claimed it for his forthcoming expenses in Miami.

Almost all our support had come from the expat community of Europeans and Americans who owned most of the businesses and basically ran the place. The indifference of the locals, descendants of African slaves and comprising ninety per cent of the population, was intimated by a carload of them who pulled up beside me as I walked to Turtle Cove the last morning.

"Yo' not welcome here," said one, a big fatty bulging out of the passenger window of the red Datsun Sunny. All the glass was missing, and gangsta rap was thudding from the back seat. "Why tone choo go back home?"

I resisted the temptation to conduct a quick history lesson, pointing out that if it hadn't been for the extermination of the former indigenous people, the Lucayan Taino, shortly after Columbus's arrival, I could well ask the same of him.

"Why don't *you* fuck off?" I said instead, immediately wishing I hadn't. Any one of the brutes was big enough to flatten my head between giant, baseball mitt-sized paws, and the road was deserted.

"Yo' bedda apologize muthafucka!" shrieked the driver, head popping out tortoise-like where the windscreen should have been. "O' we gonna spred yo' face all over da road!"

I was alone. Easy prey. Like a pack of hunting dogs, they began to tail me, baying at my heels. All I could do was keep walking, eyes fixed firmly ahead, cursing my big mouth and trying not to look as terrified as I felt. Any second it would come. A knife in the back. A bullet. A bottle. *Just what I need after pedalling all this way,* I muttered to myself, *getting bumped off by Provo's answer to the Boo-Yaa T.R.I.B.E. in the middle of Bumblefuck Nowhere.**

---

*   Sumo-sized LA hip hop group descended from American Samoa.

After a few minutes, the thugs thankfully tired of their bullying, and sped off in a sputtering cloud of fumes to find somebody else to intimidate.

Of course, this was just one bad encounter in hundreds if not thousands of good ones. Our most enthusiastic supporters came in the form of Barbara and Chuck Hesse, owners of the world-renowned Caicos Conch Farm, which we visited our final afternoon. It was a blissful interlude of overlapping delights, starting with the drive across the island in the back of Barbara's pickup. The feeling of speed was immense, cool air splashing across our faces as we zoomed past gaily-coloured houses, and skipping gangs of neatly dressed children sprung from the Baptist churches. Tropical birdsong and exotic fragrances from roadside blossoms blended seamlessly from one to the next.

At the end of our tour, Barbara presented us with one of the magnificent queen conch shells. In time, it would become an expedition treasure. Just as the boys had used one to call their meetings in *Lord of the Flies*, so we would use ours to herald the start and end of future voyages with a single, high-pitched blast.

The only disappointment before setting off the next morning was the story of our non-biodegradable rubbish. Ten trash bags filled with plastic and cans had been hauled off for recycling. Feeling rather pleased with our efforts, we asked Barbara where the recycling plant was. She laughed, pointing out to sea.

"They'll just tow it out on a barge with all the rest of the garbage from the island and dump it. The sea is the only recycling plant we have around here."[*]

Steve and I looked at each other in disbelief. All those nights rolling

---

[*]   According to the Marine Resource Conservation working group of the Asia-Pacific Economic Cooperation (APEC), 6.4 million tons of human refuse reaches the world's oceans each year, three times as much as the weight of fish caught. More than half of this is plastic, killing up to one million sea birds, 100,000 sea mammals, and countless fish annually.

around in the stern compartment with piles of stinking rubbish, thinking we were doing the right thing not polluting the ocean. All for nothing!

WAVING A LAST farewell through the hatch, Steve steered *Moksha* through the narrow channel snaking from the marina, and headed for open water. Being high tide we cleared the reef easily, and set a northwesterly course for Miami, leaving Cuba to the south, and the Bahamas to the north.

Aside from mild queasiness and occasional clumsiness—a spoon dropped over the side, the odd missed handhold leading to a smashed head or shoulder—the first few days back on board were like chalk and cheese to the zombie-like state we'd arrived in. For the time being at least, we were fresh and alert. Staying awake for the graveyard shifts posed no problem. Even levering in and out of the Rathole could be done in a single movement, our arms having regained much of their former strength.

With two weeks until Miami, I resumed my wilderness immersion programme, formalizing the requisite method of inquiry for ultimate truth into a new discipline. Critical Eye was a way of looking at the world with fresh eyes, using One Pointed Attention to see past the agents of truth—words, images, symbols, and formulas—to the pure, subjective experience hidden beneath. As a human I instinctively copied memes, elements of culture such as ideas, habits, values, and beliefs spread by non-genetic means, then sat back and allowed them to remain largely unaltered regardless of changing circumstances. It was by an almost deliberate act of denial that I conveniently overlooked how these systems are open to constant reassessment, revision, and improvement. Blind acceptance offered the perfect conditions for redundant practises and untruths to take hold. Therefore, I had a *duty* to scrutinize the superficial reality of the world around me. Not least because, as

Critical Eye reminded me, "I," in a sense, created it, attaching pre-conditioned labels to electrochemical signals conveyed through the five senses.

On a practical level aboard *Moksha*, I could use Critical Eye to improve aspects of life aboard. Peter Bird's vent was one. The enclosed cockpit had turned into an oven since reaching the tropics. Wind blowing from any direction other than directly astern would skim over the top of the vent, with a negligible amount actually going in. Retrieving one of the PVC collision mats, I carved out a custom section and wedged it at a forty-five degree angle above the vent. The makeshift deflector could be swivelled to face whichever direction the wind was coming from, diverting a cooling breeze onto the pedaller's head any time day or night.

I imagined Critical Eye improving life on land, too. A dripping tap could be fixed in a few minutes with a fifty pence washer, conserving thousands of gallons a year.* And bicycling or walking, as opposed to using the car, would save money, improve health and fitness, and reduce carbon emissions.

On a wider, more philosophical level, I employed Critical Eye to identify memes incompatible with a sustainable human presence on Earth. As a warm-blooded organism, I needed a certain amount of food, water, shelter, and energy to survive. Beyond these thresholds, however, and beyond a corresponding increase in wellbeing, I became part of the problem as a consumer, not part of the solution.

These were the things I mulled as I pedalled. For, as Shakespeare noted in *Twelfth Night*, "no prisons are more confining than those we know not we are in." Critical Eye was a bid to wrest back present and future realities from so-called fate, steering destiny by conscious design, rather than being at the mercy of it.

---

* A single faucet leaking sixty drops a minute wastes 2,082 gallons a year.

SOMETIMES, HOWEVER, FATE sticks its oar in whether you like it or not. Our heading took us past Hogsty reef, last resting place of scores of run aground hulks. It had to happen, of course. It was sod's law. A mile north of the reef, the gearbox froze.

"Unbelievable!" Steve groaned, "Why didn't that guy do the job properly for fuck's sake?"

It was the bearings again—at least that's what it felt like. The cranks would turn. The mechanism would seize. Three or four minutes later, the problem would resolve itself enough to resume pedalling. The cycle would then be repeated.

All the time we were losing ground against the north wind. It wouldn't be long before we were put onto the rocks.

Panic set in. Holes hadn't yet been cut in the side of the cabin to deploy the oars. Steve started rifling through the toolkit for the wire saw, muttering furiously. "If you want something done right, you've gotta do it yourself!"

For once, I agreed. If we'd had a sledgehammer, I would have gladly smashed the gearbox to a thousand pieces. Fortunately we didn't, so I turned my attention to untying the oars instead. The knots had welded with salt, proving too tight to loosen even with pliers. Precious seconds ticked by. Steve wasn't faring much better with the oar holes. He was only halfway through the first one, his hands covered in blood from the wire saw cutting into his fingers. The situation looked desperate.

Sitting back in the pedal seat, I took a deep breath, and tried to calm my overheated brain, also in danger of seizing. There had to be another way. Looking at the problem with fresh eyes was what was needed, the Critical Eye method of seeing past the label of "gearbox" to the underlying form.

The clues were in the symptoms. In addition to the stop-start pattern, the unit was getting hot. This suggested friction at play, possibly from the bearings. But Steve had pumped a few shots of grease into the newly installed grease point only that morning. Had he put in too much? Or maybe it wasn't the bearings at all. Maybe one of the sprockets had worked out of alignment...

I let my thoughts drift sideways, allowing the subconscious to ruminate on other, less obvious possibilities. My gaze came to rest on the A-frame holding the cranks. Grease was oozing from the bottom bracket—we always kept it crammed. What if the gearbox just needed the same treatment?

The reef was now less than a hundred yards away, crashing waves sending plumes of water rocketing into the air. The time for thinking was over. Sliding the pedal seat forward and opening the rear bulkhead, I slithered head first into the stern compartment. Somewhere in amongst all that chaos was a replacement grease cartridge.

I heard a loud *SNAP!* followed by "bugger the thing!" The wire saw had broken. Rowing ourselves off the rocks was no longer an option. All hope now rested in the gearbox.

After a minute of frantic rummaging, I found the tube of grease under George's pornography, and threw it to Steve.

Quickly now...

He loaded the grease gun, and began frantically pumping. "Nothing doing," he said in frustration. "Must be an airlock... *Fuck!*"

The rocks were getting closer. Each wave collided with the bevelled edge of the reef, erupting in a boiling mass.

Take out cartridge... Repeat procedure...

Grease was everywhere, on our hands, legs, and the pedal seat. We took it in turns to pump. Grease at last began curling from the edges of the gearbox.

Now for the test...

Pushing the seat back into position, I tried pedalling. My heart was thumping and blood pounded in my ears. *Any second now, I'll feel the telltale tightening followed by a full-on seize...* We picked up speed. I threw the rudder hard over, steering away from the reef. Thirty long seconds went by. Still the cranks turned smoothly.

Two minutes… Three minutes… Five…

We were back in business.

FOUR DAYS LATER, February 8, the wind freshened to force 5 and backed to the northwest, straight on the nose. The shipping forecast on medium wave reported a massive storm two hundred miles to the north, with waves as high as sixty-nine feet. The tail end of it would reach us by nightfall.

We altered course to 330 degrees, almost due north, to pre-empt the wind and waves that would soon start driving us south. As the afternoon wore on and the wind speed increased, *Moksha* began to buck and heave in the mounting swell, straining to turn beam-on. Even with the tiller hard to starboard, it was a battle just to maintain our position; we were effectively pedalling on the spot. Still, it was better than throwing out the car tyres and being pushed any nearer the Cuban coast, now only twenty miles away. If we got too close, *Moksha* would likely be impounded—assuming we weren't shipwrecked first.

It was the hardest pedalling of the voyage so far. *Punch forward… Punch forward… Punch forward…* became my motivational mantra, borrowed from our expedition president, Sir Ranulph Fiennes, who'd used a similar maxim to keep plodding across Antarctica a year previously. To ease the pressure on our knees, we changed shifts every hour instead of every two. Each wave rolling in from the north swallowed the entire front half of the boat, flinging torrents of water through the ventilation hatch and into the pedaller's lap. The regular drenchings had a welcome cooling effect on our overheated bodies, but by morning, the chafing in my groin had become unbearable. After a brief interlude, the saltwater boils were back with a vengeance. They were popping up everywhere this time: balls, arse, behind the knees, elbows, and thighs.

Something had to be done.

Tearing a three-inch wide strip of canvas from the old sail bag, I rigged up a makeshift testicle harness. The "Plumb Line," as it became known, formed a big looping cradle secured by two lengths of shock cord to the roof above the pedal seat. This elevated my balls a good four inches above their customary position, and despite swinging awkwardly like a meat pendulum on the piss, the friction problem was at least solved. The harness also stymied a recent hatch of maggots nesting in the pedal seat, gorging themselves on the blood and pus from our salt sores. Only that morning, one had tried to burrow its way into my left testicle, possibly mistaking it for a rotten plum.

Later that morning, I spotted breakers on a reef some three miles off our forward port quarter. A quick bearing with the handheld compass put the reef at 275 degrees, but the chart had the one-fathom shallows marked at 320. Was the chart wrong?

Steve stopped pedalling and joined me in the open hatchway. Straining into the glare, he watched the belt of white water rolling eastwards like surf breaking along a beach. "That's not a reef. It's a speedboat!"

Sure enough, the craft altered course, heading straight for us. Returning to the pedal seat, Steve grabbed the VHF handset and requested the mystery vessel to state its intention. No response. This was the first bad sign. The second, evident as the unmarked forty-foot motorcruiser drew near, was the semi-automatics brandished by the six men standing along the rail. They were unshaven, desperate-looking, and none were in uniform.

"Here we go," I murmured, my voice shaking slightly. "I think we're about to get rolled by pirates."

I stopped filming, and hid the new video camera inside the Rathole along with the binoculars and the Nikon still camera. Steve kept pedalling, cautiously extracting a magazine of hand flares from one of the RAF lifejackets, and placing it under his right elbow. Not that we could do much against such odds, but if things got really nasty, the rocket-style flares were our only defence.

One of the pirates started screaming in Spanish. Not understanding a word, we hollered back in English, which they didn't understand either. One thing quite clear, however, judging by how increasingly agitated they were getting—stabbing their guns in the air and waving their free arms like demented traffic wardens—was that they wanted us to stop.

It was too late to throw on a pair of shorts. As they readied to board, Steve and I stood up in the hatchway together.

The shouting and gun jabbing stopped immediately, replaced by stunned silence. Our would-be buccaneers wore expressions ranging from open-mouthed dismay to utter revulsion. Perhaps they'd been expecting a nice easy target, a luxury yacht charter with wealthy holidaymakers on board. Instead, they'd apparently flagged down a souped-up pedalo manned by a pair of buck-naked homos covered in suppurating sores, and sweating like two kiddy fiddlers in court. The grinning one in the multi-coloured safari hat was clearly insane. The other had a giant bird's nest attached to the lower part of his face.

Fearing the diseases we undoubtedly carried, the skipper scowled in disgust, gunned his engine, and roared back towards Cuba.

February 10
SHORTLY BEFORE DAWN, two cruise ships the size of housing estates passed a mile to the south, ploughing up the deep-water corridor towards the Florida Keys. All ships bound for the US were now forced through this bottleneck. We preferred our chances on the Great Bahama Bank far-

ther to the north. It was the most surreal, breathtaking body of water we'd yet pedalled across, a liquid veneer just fifteen-feet deep in places, covering a thick slab of coral reef limestone deposited in the Cretaceous period. The shallowness would keep the lethal leviathans out of our path.

Whoever was on break could typically be found splayed over the foredeck, gazing down through the translucent depths, mesmerized by a shimmering carpet of perfectly chiselled sand, ribbed and fluted like the undulating remains of some prehistoric sea creature. Black starfish stuck motionless to the seabed. The odd gambolling dorado and screeching gull were the only other evidence of life. And once, lying in the Rathole in the early hours, I heard a pod of dolphins approaching in the darkness:

Spff-tah… Spff-tah… Spff-tah… The short shallow gasps were amplified through the wooden hull as they surfaced for air. Then, the deep *Spff-taah!* of the last breath before the next dive, passing right underneath the sleeping compartment, and continuing northwards.

The wind dropped, and the heat became almost unbearable. We sweated continuously day and night. The only thing that seemed to flourish in such loathsome conditions was our equally loathsome maggot colony, invigorated by the complement of sweat to their already high protein diet. When the foam padding in the pedal seat started wriggling like a corpse, I made up a five-to-one solution of chlorine-based biocide, the fungicide normally used to kill biological growth inside the water maker. The maggots responded with enthusiasm, waggling their rice-sized bodies at me hungrily, as if to say, *"Please sir, I want some more!"*

Exasperated, I poured it on full strength.

"That should fry the little fuckers," muttered Steve, his expression a mixture of horror and morbid fascination.

"Yep. Strong enough to sizzle the arse off a rhinoceros."

Sure enough, the wriggling stopped a few seconds later.

Diving into our own private swimming pool stretching for hundreds of square miles was the prize waiting at the end of each sweltering pedal shift. There, braced beneath the hull where the water was coldest, letting your head be rolled between the gentle palms of the current, temples massaged with expert dexterity, the body quickly chilled to a tolerable operating temperature. Pure heaven. The stifling Rathole was duly supplanted by this "new favourite place to be."

Inside the airless cockpit, I sought distraction in the Created Value task of making a flag for our arrival. Once finished, the three-by-two-foot piece of canvas would read: "We Need a Sponsor!" The fifteen letters crudely fashioned from my last tee shirt each took an hour to sew, but that was fine. They were fifteen hours of otherwise mindless torture that flew by as I pedalled.

Steve volunteered to wave the flag at the scores of media helicopters buzzing all around as we made our triumphant entry into Miami.

AFTER A WEEK of favourable if hard-earned progress, we neared the northern edge of the Great Bahama Bank. Another 48 hours, and we'd be in Miami.

With Florida's sagging buttock so close we could almost reach out and spank it, I'd all but given up hope of peeling back the last layers of the onion to reveal so-called "ultimate truth." No matter how long I meditated during my graveyard shifts, or how diligently I applied Critical Eye to the world around me, I just couldn't seem to break through. It was like straining to see one of those three-dimensional images embedded in a two-dimensional picture. The more I forced it, the more elusive the face of the Madonna, the Mona Lisa, or whatever was supposedly hidden, became.

Absolute truth is just another illusion… I wrote in my journal. And in the early hours of day 109, I threw in the towel, resigning myself in the words of the Buddha to remain "a herdsmen of other men's cows."*

Then, towards the end of my second graveyard shift, something inside me tripped. I felt increasingly light-headed, my body filling with energy like static building before a storm. By the time I slipped into the Rathole at first light, dripping in sweat, staring up at the roof of the narrow compartment, my mind was racing. After fifteen minutes of chaotic, random thought, something tangible began to take shape. At first all I saw was an acorn in the ground, germinating slowly in time-lapse: roots thrusting downwards, a single shoot sprouting up through the soil. The fledging stalk picked up momentum, pushing skyward, taking the form of a sapling with branches, leaves, and tiny flowering buds. Soon, a full-grown oak tree stood before me, swaying gently in the breeze. It was strong and self-sufficient, all alone in a sunlit meadow, completely independent of its surroundings.

Things metamorphosed from simple botany. I noticed the subtle exchanges going on around the tree, the photosynthesis between the leaves and the air, and the nutrient and water transfer between the roots and the earth. The oak wasn't separate at all, I realized. It was intrinsically linked to everything around it, even to the birds using its canopy for shade, and the tiny insects roaming its bark for food.

Faster and faster, my mind began travelling at lightning speed, following the threads of connectivity: molecules of oxygen released from a stoma in the underside of a leaf, up into the atmosphere where they combined with hydrogen and dust particles, falling back down to Earth as rain hammering on the parched land. The rain formed a trickle, growing to a stream, swelling to a river flowing to the sea. A woman stooped by the water's edge to fill a bucket. Raising it to her head, she began walking back to her village to start the family meal…

---

*   Relying on the direct experiences of others for knowledge and understanding of truth.

On and on went the train of connections, until the oak tree appeared once again. Except something was different. A shimmering glow, radiant like a heat mirage, blurred the trunk and the leaves, bleeding the edges into the ether. Any distinction between the tree and its surroundings gradually dissipated. The two merged as one, a molten mass of photons and electrons, flowing golden and incandescent. The former label of "tree" no longer existed. It was simply a vessel through which life flowed.

The interconnectedness of all things became overwhelming. I opened my eyes and saw the same energy streaming where the solid outline of the sleeping compartment had been. It was like the phosphorescence we'd seen at night, swirling and spinning in the wake of cavorting dolphins. Only it was now intrinsic to everything. In essence, it *was* everything. I raised my hand and saw the same river of light. As a human, I, too, was merely a vessel through which life flowed.

Then it hit me.

At the core of all life is similarity, a common chemistry. The differences in the world around me and their sensory expressions—colours, smells, textures, tastes, sounds, and so on—were all constructs of the mind, illusions, the product of a prolonged evolutionary process whereby humans have made sense out of chaos.

Even the "I" of Jason Lewis was just an identikit collection of tags fashioned by consciousness, projecting a seemingly tangible self: dark hair, green eyes, pale skin, English, apolitical, agnostic, and so on. At a molecular level, the enduring "I" was made up of the same underlying chemistry as a chair, caterpillar, or oak tree. The more attached people get to their labels, and the longer they go without questioning them, the more distance put between the illusory I, and the real "I" - nature itself.

The Great Fall of man...

Something shifted. Instead of following its habitual linear trajectory, the narrative comprising consciousness began expanding in all directions, crystallizing everything in its path like ice forming in water. The single point of view became many, a multi-screened cineplex where I could watch all the films at the same time. Subjectivity in turn merged with objectivity, and the "I" became akin to a mirror illuminating all things as mere reflections and patterns of itself—pure energy. In this way, every process in the universe became instantly recognizable, and therefore instantly knowable. Not only was the "I" every*where* at the same time, the "I" was every*thing* at the same time, from the tiniest quark to the farthest galaxy. It was like a homecoming, the ultimate state of equilibrium.

Then the second Aha!

Everything in life can be understood as a variation of itself...

This must be where the likes of Poincaré and Einstein came for their intuitive insights into the workings of the cosmos, I told myself. But to share it with others, they needed metaphors. Only through the language of mathematics could Einstein's theory of relativity formally exist.

It was the final piece of the puzzle I'd been searching for. The links between analogies offered an interconnected roadmap of *potential* understanding of all phenomena. But they were only pathways to truth, not ultimate truth itself. As trail markers, they only took you so far. Beyond a certain point, you were on your own.

I felt another shift, after which I have no recollection, as a separate mind to intellectualize with ceased to exist. The observer and observed had become one. It was all one piece, unbroken, whole. Months later, someone explained this was known as a state of non-dualism in the West, or *Samadhi* for Hindus and Buddhists in the East. In short, a brief glimpse of *Moksha*, or enlightenment.

I came down from the molecular plane some time later, sucked back through the wormhole of space-time into dualistic awareness, able once again to rationalize experience. And the normal way of looking at the world seemed so monochrome and drab by comparison.

When I shared the experience with Steve over breakfast, he looked amused more than anything. Apart from being focused on our arrival in the US, he probably thought my head was pretty well cooked by this point in the voyage. Besides, how do you respond to someone telling you they've just snatched a peek at the divine?

SWEEPING ACROSS THE swift-flowing Gulf Stream towards Biscayne Bay, the pace of life aboard accelerated with landfall imminent. Any semblance of mental clarity lingering from the *Samadhi* was swept aside in a swarming barrage of logistical considerations: the planned rendezvous with Kenny outside Fowey Rocks, finishing the sponsorship flag, the impending media frenzy…

Steve was already a blur of activity, tying on lines to throw, requisitioning the car tyres as makeshift fenders, clearing the decks of unnecessary clutter to make *Moksha* look a little more shipshape for the television cameras.

By first light, save for one close encounter with a phantom cargo ship called *Sea Monster* that appeared out of nowhere and nearly chomped us in half, we were safely across the Straits of Florida, and waiting at the rendezvous point. Kenny would roll up any minute with an ITN camera crew and Coast Guard cutter as escort.

Miami remained obscured by a curtain of low-lying haze, but an acrid whiff on the westerly breeze left us in no doubt of its portentous proximity. Drifting gently in the lee of Fowey Rocks, we swigged the last of the Ballantine's, and congratulated each other. The first major hurdle of the circumnavigation was as good as in the bag, and we were about to become the first people in history to cross from mainland Europe to North America by human power, proving ourselves a viable sponsorship proposition for the rest of the journey. On a personal level, after months of wilderness immersion, I'd exposed the illusion of independent existence, solving the first part of my overarching quest for how to live life on a crowded planet.

But it hadn't all been positive. My introspection, and Steve's struggle with life aboard, had created a rift between us. The harsh exchange of words after the BVI mutiny still echoed in my head: *"It doesn't bode well for the remainder of the expedition…"* What had Steve really meant by this?

One thing was clear. A human-powered circumnavigation was a far more serious undertaking than I'd originally imagined. This wasn't just some drunken college caper. It really was turning out to be the ultimate human challenge, requiring every ounce of physical, emotional, and spiritual strength if we were to succeed.

NORTH AMERICA
SKATING THE DEEP SOUTH

What is life? It is the flash of a firefly in the night. It is the breath of a buffalo in the wintertime. It is the little shadow which runs across the grass and loses itself in the sunset.

—Last words of CROWFOOT, *BLACKFOOT*

We ... must come again to a moral comprehension of the earth and air. We must live according to the principle of a land ethic. The alternative is that we shall not live at all.

—NAVARRE SCOTT MOMADAY, *KIOWA-CHEROKEE*

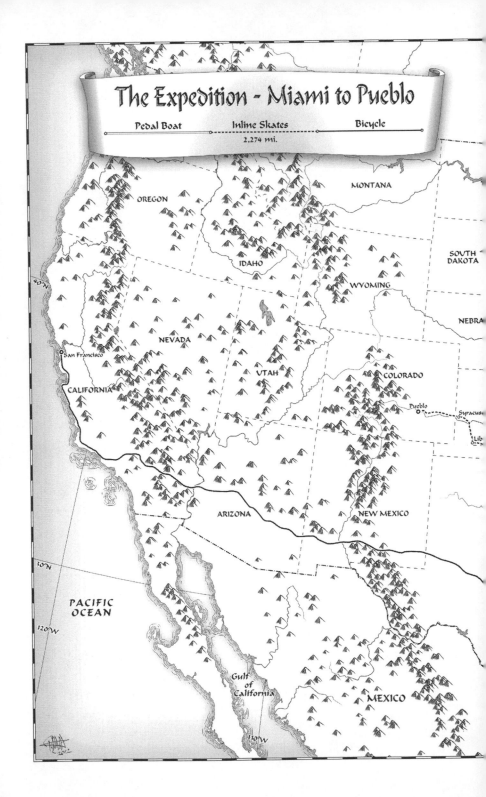

Atlantic Crossing: Day 111. Miami Arrival. February 17, 1995

I T WAS CIRCUS TIME. An *NBC* news chopper clattered overhead, and diesel fumes reeked in our nostrils from *Reel Time*, a sports fishing boat chartered by *News at Ten* to shadow our final approach. Steve stood aloft, proudly displaying our "We Need A Sponsor!" flag for the cameras. On the skyline, Miami's financial district loomed like a rambling graveyard of misshapen headstones. After the fluid forms of the ocean void, the orchestrated symmetry of human architecture looked alien and unearthly, all lines, lines, lines…

There were no treacherous reefs to cross this time, no mischievous sirens calling to us from shore. Just a baffling maze of channels to navigate before reaching our final destination, the Miami Yacht Club, where the main body of press would be waiting. Fortunately, the US Coast Guard cutter was guiding us the last few miles, which turned out to be the most tortuous of the entire voyage. Five minutes felt like an hour. An hour a lifetime.

Then, one last bridge, traffic thundering over the gridiron plates above us, one last corner, and there it was, the clubhouse surrounded by a sea of masts bristling at the sky like a hairbrush. A lone pontoon symbolized our journey's end.

But something wasn't right.

As I sat cross-legged on the cabin roof, Steve pedalling the last hundred yards, a distinct aura of unease radiated from the surprisingly small number of people standing on the wooden jetty. I could make out Kenny, his camera levelled at the ready, and Martin and Catriona, who had both flown over to help organize press. Stuart was there, grinning like a cat as usual and clutching his customary bottle of champagne. Indeed, a fatuous grin appeared fixed on every face.

Where the blazes were the TV cameras and journalists?

Moksha bumped up alongside the jetty. I threw a line to Kenneth Crutchlow, Director of the Ocean Rowing Society. At the same time

Stuart popped the cork—a little too enthusiastically. A modest plume erupted, missed the boat completely, and landed in the water with a resounding *FLOP!*

The light clapping was interrupted by a loud, *"Yeehaaaa!"* from Steve, who leapt up from the pedal seat and grabbed the bottle from his father. Then it was all over. No flashing cameras. No barging television crews. Later we learned a reporter and photographer had turned up from the *Biscayne Bay Tribune*, but fled like rats from a sinking ship upon learning they comprised the entire press corps.

Concealing my embarrassment, I stepped onto the swaying pontoon and started pumping every hand in sight. It didn't take long.

"Is someone getting married?" asked an elderly woman. She had a New Jersey accent, bleached hair, and pink cat eye specs, possibly a snowbird escaping the freezing Northeast winter.

"Not exactly," I replied. "This is err...We've just um..."

The words dried on my tongue. It struck me that what I was about to say would sound utterly ridiculous to the average person wondering what all the fuss was about. *"We've just pedalled across the Atlantic..."* She'd think I was taking the piss. Perhaps that was why no press had turned up?

And so, within a minute of completing a 5,641 mile, 111-day crossing of the Atlantic Ocean, I found myself having a perfectly normal conversation with Joan, a complete stranger, about Boo-Boo, her sick cat.

"Boo-Boo just doesn't seem to be eating well at the moment," she said anxiously.

"Oh. That must be worrying."

"Yes it is. Actually, I took him to the vet yesterday, but they said there's nothing wrong with him."

"Maybe it's a hair-ball?"

"Oh no, I'm very careful about keeping his coat clean. I brush him three times a day!" She lifted her glasses to dab her eyes. They were watering, either from the glare off the water, or the worry of Boo-Boo not eating properly.

"Does he have long hair?" I asked.

Joan shook her head. "No. He's a shorthaired Charteux. Are you familiar?"

"No, I don't believe so."

"Oooh! They're beautiful animals. Date back to sixteenth century France you know…"

THE MYSTERY OF the press disaster revealed itself later that afternoon. After a week of phone bashing, our PR team had sent out the final press release to seven hundred television stations, print media, and radio programmes countrywide. It was a well-crafted, succinct one pager, hitting all the major points—bar one. There were no fewer than seven Miami Yacht Clubs in the area, and they hadn't specified which one.

THE NEXT MORNING, Stuart drove us to the first day of the boat show. Frame by frame, America unfurled itself through the open windows as a stream of polychromatic snapshots: flashing neon above a liquor store, peeling billboards advertising Banana Blueberry Yoghurt Cake, bums swigging Colt 45 malt beer on the sidewalk, *Silence of the Lambs* playing on a television set in the petrol station kiosk. All of it was lacquered in a veneer of restless energy, the lifeblood of opportunity drip-feeding the American Dream. The task of not just surviving but raising £24,000 in such a terrifying place struck me as daunting in the extreme.

True to American form, opportunity knocked on our door, too—albeit one I would have traded for pedalling back across the Atlantic any day of the week. Within the hour, Stuart had us trussed like turkeys in crisp new expedition tee shirts, and stationed on a virtual leash within ten feet of *Moksha.* Our VIP stand was the car park next to the Jewish cemetery. In spite of the dubious location, a steady stream of punters ambled up, either seduced by *Moksha's* peculiar shape complete with two-inch barnacles still clinging to her hull, or herded forcibly by Stuart. As "The guys who had now done it," Steve and I were on hand to field questions and wax lyrical about the voyage.

"What was the biggest storm?"

"How high was the highest wave?"

"Best and worst moments?"

In America, it was all ests, ests, ests.

"Did you get eaten by any sharks?" one man asked without batting an eye.

Clearly not, you fucking idiot, I almost said. *Otherwise, I wouldn't be standing here talking to you, now would I?* Exercising restraint, I bit my tongue instead. For whether it was flying fish, giant waves, or man-eating sharks—rather the lack thereof—the crux of every circuitous conversation ultimately boiled down to one thing. Whether $20 could be extracted from a victim's wallet for a signed tee shirt, or their name added to *Moksha's* hull in vinyl letters.

As a salesperson, I was useless. "You've got to cut to the chase quicker," Stuart would hiss at my shoulder, after catching me boring the pants off yet another prospective customer with the intricacies of human consciousness. "If they don't fork out the readies in a couple of minutes then, *BAM,* on to the next!"

He was right, of course, but I wrestled with the calculated intent of it all. The average American was too trusting; it was like clubbing baby seals. There was none of the sneering cynicism or muted suspicion that made each hard-won sale at the London Boat Show a year earlier seem a victory of divine justice. No tightwads picking at loose threads on the tee shirts, angling for a discount. No haggling over the price of a vinyl name. In contrast to the parsimonious Brits, Americans were imbued with something rather special. That a dream, whether your own or anybody else's, is a birthright, sacrosanct and untouchable. And if you have one, "Then go for it!" they would say, and really mean it.

It was an attitude that had built a country.

Perhaps this was why the owner of a local telecommunications company, Richard Pudsey, offered an interest-free loan of $2,000 to print our first run of four hundred tee shirts, repayable whenever possible. And why Nancy Sanford, a pedal power enthusiast, volunteered to take a week from her job as a hotel manager in St Petersburg, and travel 500 miles to help out at the boat show.

With $600 in the kitty by the end of the first day, we were all in agreement. The expedition might just survive in a place like America.

March 22, Sunrise Middle School, Fort Lauderdale

"So, HOW DO you go to the bathroom?" asked a pretty girl with strawberry blonde pigtails sitting at the front of the class. One of her companions had asked the question earlier, but at the risk of never getting through the rest of the half hour presentation—the answer unfailingly produced pandemonium—I'd ignored it. The entire sixth grade class looked at me imploringly. They'd heard about the whale with the itchy back, Lolita the Lure, and *Moksha* capsizing. What they really wanted to know was how we took a dump.

I sighed. "Stu, can you do the honours this time?" It was only the fifth time we'd been asked the same question by as many classes that morning.

Clambering onto the teacher's desk and hanging his backside over the edge, Stuart proceeded to give an admirable demonstration of the toilet arrangements aboard *Moksha*. As predicted, the class erupted—thirty children shrieking in ear-splitting unison.

"Eeuuuuwww!!"

A month had passed since the boat show, where we'd raised a respectable $6,000. But after reimbursing Martin, Catriona, and Kenny, all of whom had returned to England—in Kenny's case to edit a one-hour documentary for Discovery Europe—the balance was only enough to pay off Richard Pudsey. Then there was the prohibitive cost of living in Miami. What we really needed was a mid-sized town, one large enough to network and build recognition, but not so big that it consumed us.

And so, a week after the show, *Moksha* was slipped back into the protected waters of the Intracoastal Waterway, and pedalled twenty-five miles up the coast to Fort Lauderdale. This time we made sure the exact location of our arrival was printed in bold at the bottom of the press release. The next morning, a front-page article appeared in *The Sun Sentinel*, triggering a follow-on feature in the *Miami Herald Tribune* who, ironically, had missed us the first time around in Miami.

Once the story had legs, things really started to roll. Dr Richard Harris, a local psychologist, volunteered an office at his practice in nearby Plantation. Kelly and Neil Lawrence offered the spare bedroom in their home, and space in the backyard to park *Moksha*. Kimberli Swann, another local resident, helped arrange school visits.

Stuart and I joined forces, hauling *Moksha* around to festivals, boat shows, and flea markets, indeed any venue with warm bodies to sell merchandize to, even street parties. We worked well together, neither one having to pull rank over the other. When we visited schools, which we always did for free, Stuart assumed the role of showman, leaving me to concentrate on teasing out educational aspects of the journey.

Steve, meanwhile, focused his efforts giving slide shows to yacht clubs, Rotary, and Kiwanis Clubs. Since his mother and ex-girlfriend had stumped up most of the original loan, he was driven by an added sense of urgency to repay the money as quickly as possible. But after a month of relentless fundraising, the stress was starting to show. He looked exhausted and withdrawn. It seemed a cruel paradox that after all those months at sea dreaming of terra firma, life on land was turning out to be no less of a grind.

"Okay!" I shouted over the chattering children. "Who wants to be a crewmember on *Moksha?*"

A sea of hands shot into the air, accompanied by a chorus of shrill voices. *"Me! Me! Me! Me! Me!"*

As ringmaster, Stuart took over. "Alright, settle down now. Form a single line by the door, please."

The old Pied Piper led the skipping children to where *Moksha* was parked outside the front entrance. The first four-person crew comprised the girl with the blonde pigtails as captain; her best friend, a shy girl with specs, as first mate; a frizzy-haired boy as the bosun; and his plump sidekick with ginger freckles as the cook. For the next few minutes, the children were free to explore the inside of the boat: sliding in and out of the Rathole, taking readings off the compass, frying up imaginary flying fish on the stove, even pedalling, the propeller spinning freely underneath. Stuart stood on the starboard gunwale, firing off instructions and cracking jokes. Being a big kid himself, he was in his element.

"Now, do you remember when Jason told you about the Rogue Wave?"

The crew nodded eagerly. The class before had already told them what happened next. Stuart and I took our places either side of the cockpit.

"Ready?" Stuart hollered. "Altogether now, *SURFINGGGGGGG!!*"

Delighted squeals filled the air as we rocked *Moksha* back and forth as hard as we could, re-enacting the final moments before the now infamous capsize.

While Stuart picked out the next crew, I fielded questions from the rest of the class. Up went two hands from a pair of giggling girls.

"Do you have a girlfriend?" asked one.

Crikey! I thought. *These American kids aren't shy are they?*

Recovering my composure, I said, "No. It probably wouldn't be fair expecting someone back home to wait for so long, now would it?"

The girls looked coyly at their feet.

"You ask him," one whispered.

"No, you!" hissed the other.

Finally, the more confident of the two looked me straight in the eye, and said, "Would you like one?"

The class erupted once again. I opened my mouth to reply, and then closed it again. Words had completely failed me.

Four and a half months later…

TWO THINGS RULED my every waking move. A list entitled, *People To Call.* Another, *Things To Do.* My life had effectively transmuted into a Filofax, a leather-bound Lernaean Hydra sprouting two entries for every one struck off. But following a moment of absentmindedness, my "life" was now heading south towards the Keys carried by a stiff breeze. Earlier in the day, Stuart and I had taken *Moksha* to a kids reading festival hosted by the Broward County Library. We'd driven off at the end with the Filofax on *Moksha's* roof.

Chasing the fluttering sheets down Federal Highway, I realized how subjugated I'd become. For the first few weeks in Fort Lauderdale, I'd managed to preserve some mental clarity from the voyage, sleeping on a plot of wooded land near Neil and Kelly's, rising early to meditate and practise Critical Eye. But such grounding episodes with nature petered out as the calendar filled with engagements. Objective reality began wending its way back into my head like a weed, reasserting control over my daily affairs.

Dr Harris had voiced something similar in his office the previous evening. He and his family had just returned from a camping trip to Oregon, and his feet were still itchy. "I don't think I can live in Fort Lauderdale much longer," he said wearily. "All this concrete. I can't stand it anymore."

He was staring out of the window at the lifeless parking lot. "Only a decade ago this was all everglades, teeming with life. Now look at it." He ran his fingers through his greying hair, and sighed.

It was hard to imagine the town of Plantation as anything different to what it was: one giant slab of concrete covered with offices and strip malls.

"I wish I was free like you, Jason. Able to just pick up and leave whenever I felt like it."

This was not the time, I decided, to disillusion him further explaining how shackled I was by expedition debt, so I voiced the obvious. "Why don't you just move the family to Oregon, Rick?"

"I would in a heartbeat. Only thing is, I make my living out of— how should I say this—people being fucked up in the head, you see?"

I didn't.

"People don't get fucked up in Oregon," he continued. "At least not like they do here in southeast Florida. People are outside more, in the wild, behaving like humans are meant to—using their minds *and* their bodies together. Not just spending eight hours in an office, two more in traffic, then sitting on their asses for the rest of the evening watching Jerry Springer."

I saw his dilemma. *Concrete.* It was fast becoming ours, too.

A WEEK LATER, Steve, Stuart, and I met to discuss our options over a pint at The Falcon, a British pub on University Avenue. Steve kicked things off by taking stock of our efforts. "We've thrown about five and a half grand at the debt." His eyes were bloodshot, and his fingernails nibbled down to the quick. "Another twenty to go."

Stuart returned from the bar with a round of Boddingtons, and pulled up a stool.

"Well, all I know," I muttered darkly, "is if one more person asks whether sharks attacked us on the Atlantic, I'm going to turn into one myself and bite their bloody head off!" I looked at Steve and shook my head. "I don't know how much longer I can take this."

Steve had been adamant about paying back every penny before continuing, but at the rate we were going, it would take another two years of fundraising. The debt would be cleared, but we'd be sick of the expedition, and even sicker of each other.

"Mind you," interjected Stuart. "If you throw in the towel now, it could take a lifetime to pay it all back working for three pound an hour back in England."

He was right. Ironically, the only way out of debt was to continue the expedition. Maybe we'd crack the elusive sponsorship nut in San Francisco? The PR potential of my bid to be the first person to inline skate across the US might help.

It had been a fleeting whim on the Atlantic, one I'd given more serious thought to after studying the migratory patterns of bronze-legged beauties gliding up and down Miami's South Beach boardwalk. As well as setting a record, I was interested to see how different modes of human power altered the experience of travel. We'd already used bikes in Europe, and a pedal-powered boat for the Atlantic. Would rollerblades, as unconventional as they were, be a catalyst for new experience and adventure in small-town America? It would help test a theory, that the slower you move, and the more unorthodox the means of locomotion, the richer the journey. People are more inquisitive, more likely to engage in conversation, revealing a more authentic picture of a culture's underbelly.

Early on, I'd asked Steve if he fancied the idea.

"Sod that for a game of soldiers!" was the knee-jerk response. Later, however, after considering it more thoroughly, he explained how much he loved the freedom of his bike, the larger wheels allowing impromptu off-road detours from the busy highways—impossible on skate wheels.

In The Falcon, the lunchtime crowd had thinned, and the background buzz of conversation started to ebb. Steve drained his glass. "I suppose we'll just have to ask our creditors to hang on a bit longer," he said with resignation. "Only thing is Jase, how practical do you think it'll be biking and rollerblading together?"

He meant the difference in speed. But he could easily have been referring to an even greater cause for doubt, one he'd magnanimously chosen not to mention.

I'd never skated before.

STEVE AND I departed Fort Lauderdale a fortnight later, leaving Stuart a guest of the obliging Pudsey family, and *Moksha* in the capable hands of a local boatyard, Rolly Marine.* Holding on for dear life to Steve's shoulder, I took my first teetering steps along Atlantic Boulevard, heading north. *If I can do a mile on these things,* I thought, *I can do four thousand, given enough time...*

The New River Rollers, a local skate club, accompanied us the first day. It was all about technique, I quickly realized, watching the experts

---

* A question mark still hung over the means by which *Moksha* would reach the shores of the Pacific where she was needed next. Back in England, we'd explored the possibility of building an amphibious craft to use over both land and sea. But the physics of such a vehicle—something strong enough to withstand heavy seas, but light enough to pedal over mountain ranges—proved impractical.

pull effortlessly away like swans in flight formation. Their legs swayed gracefully from side to side while their upper bodies barely moved. Waddling in their wake, I tried to imitate, but all I could manage was the ugly duckling on ice, sweating and cursing in equal measure, and expending vast amounts of energy to little effect.

At Lake Worth, we cut inland towards St Petersburg. Steve cycled alongside, shielding me from being flattened along with the road kill that littered our path: armadillos, tortoises, squirrels, and racoons. His patience was humbling. He had to brave longer, hotter hours in the saddle than if we were both cycling, while carrying most of my gear.

By day three, I was managing to stay upright for a hundred yards at a time without piling off into the ditch. Even so, any conviction that rollerblading to San Francisco was still a good idea was roundly quashed by one old-timer who pulled alongside in his pickup north of Lake Okeechobee.

"Son, do ya *want* tah die?"

In his dungarees and Ford Tractor cap, it was Uncle Jesse from *The Dukes of Hazzard*.

"What makes you say that?" I replied, gasping like a beached fish. I was sweating. I was sunburnt. It was 109 degrees Fahrenheit, and ninety-six per cent humidity.

"Ya not supposed tah go down there."

I followed his gaze, squinting into the sun. "Down where?"

He nodded in the direction we were going. "Down yonder. Wherever it is ya think ya goin'."

"Why?"

"Well, ya just *can't*. They'll run ya down, see. They'll jus... run ya down."

It was the stock rant, one we'd been subjected to hundreds of times by self-righteous bores and busybodies, making us no less determined to press on regardless. On this occasion, however, there was something unnerving about the way the old curmudgeon said, *They'll jus… run ya down, see,* like he was simply voicing a given.

Nearing Tampa Bay, I was up to twenty miles a day before collapsing in a heap, sucking on a water bottle filled with electrolytes for the remainder of the afternoon. Steve, on the other hand, had barely drawn a sweat since leaving the coast. As suspected, the difference in our speeds was becoming a problem. And there was still lingering tension from the Atlantic. We'd been cramped together for too long, getting on each other's nerves for days, even weeks at a time. Five months of fundraising in Fort Lauderdale had only compounded the stress. The US offered the chance to create some much needed breathing space before reuniting for the eight-month crossing of the Pacific.

Steve chose a southerly route across country, hugging the Gulf Coast to New Orleans, then bisecting Arizona to Southern California. I would take a more mid-country trajectory, taking in the Deep South as far as Oklahoma, cutting northwest to the Kansas prairie, and crossing the Rocky Mountains in Colorado. All things being equal, we aimed to rendezvous in San Francisco mid-October before the winter snows closed the mountain passes of the Sierras.

We spent our last night together sheltering from a torrential rainstorm in a leaky garden shed next to a foul-smelling, mosquito-infested swamp. It was five-star compared to previous nights: lying under our ponchos, fully veiled like beekeepers in our mesh *"Buzz Off!"* bug suits, fighting off marauding hordes of fire ants. A rudimentary lantern— fashioned from a strip of cloth soaked in cooking oil, and wrapped around a rake handle—served as a light source, and the means to heat a pan of rainwater for rice and tea.

"I'm thinking of asking Eilbhe to come over and ride with me," Steve announced suddenly. He was forking out the contents of a can of tuna by the flickering torchlight.

"The girl you met in the South of France?"

He nodded, his silhouetted facial contours dancing and contorting against the backdrop of the hut. "It's short notice, but she's pretty impulsive."

I'd known for some time that Steve was head over heels with this girl. They'd been exchanging letters since our Miami arrival.

"Do you mind if she uses your bike?"

"No, of course not. It'll save having to ship it to the West Coast."

I was sitting on a lawn chair, gingerly peeling away strips of zinc oxide tape from my heels and shins. A bloody mass of oozing sores from the chaffing of my new skate boots lay beneath. Some of them were already infected.

Steve bent down to take a closer look. "Better get those legs looked at when we get to Nancy's."

Later, he chanced upon a can of warm beer in his rear pannier. Cracking it open, we drank to San Francisco. The rain hammered on the roof, filling the silence that hung heavily between us. Something about the act of separating felt odd, almost taboo.

Of course, there was no way of knowing that we'd be seeing each other much sooner, and in far dire circumstances.

July 21. The Rose & Crown pub. St Petersburg, Florida
"If ye ken make it across th' Atlantic in that blumin' pedalo," roared the bartender in his Scottish mother tongue, "ye ken make it tae San Francisco oan them blumin' rollerblades."

Cheers erupted from the crowd. It was barely noon, and the assembled pub clientele—mainly Scottish, English, Irish, and Welsh expatriates—were already three sheets to the wind.

Al Anderson pushed his crimson face nearer mine. "Apologies fur th' bloody racket," he continued, loud enough for everyone in the bar to hear. "Someone must hae let ay load o' Welshman in 'ere by mistake!"

A barrage of insults ensued. As we'd found in Lagos and Fort Lauderdale, expats clung to their respective heritages like cats to floating wreckage. Tribal lines ran deeper and cultural idiosyncrasies exaggerated to compensate for the vulnerability of life adrift in far-flung lands.

But this was all in good humour. Michael Morris, a fellow Englishman, presented me with a gold medal stamped with *"VICTORY!"* on behalf of the British Floridian Club.

"How thoughtful." I smiled, flattered by the rather pre-emptive faith in the outcome of my undertaking. Turning it over, the flip side read, *"Thanks for Sailing with REGENCY CRUISES."*

Never mind, it's still a nice gesture...

"We all reckon ye'll make it laddie." Al clapped a meaty paw on my shoulder. "So we might as well start celebratin' now, eh! What'll ye be havin'—pint o' Guinness?"

I really should hit the Pinellas Trail, I thought. *Get a few miles under my belt before dark...*

I turned to Nancy, an athletic woman in her early forties. She was watching the bickering islanders with the rapt expression of someone observing zoo animals. "What do you reckon, Nance?"

"Your call Jason. You're the one who has to skate across the country."

Claiming to be a tugboat in a former life, Nancy had certainly pulled out all the stops since Steve and I reached the east shore of Tampa Bay a week earlier. Waiting in the Apollo Beach Marina were three of her recreational pedal boats known as Escapades. The next morning, we'd beelined the twelve miles across the bay to St Petersburg, saving forty-five miles by road. While Steve pressed on to Tallahassee, I had stayed at the hotel Nancy managed, and nursed my feet.

Well, maybe there's time for a quick one...

Three hours later, Nancy was beginning to slur. "Don'choo you have a continent to skate across, Jason?" I, too, was sloshed. Every time we turned to leave, Al had another round of Guinness lined up on the bar.

"Oh, yeah, thash right. That big ol'… America thingamajig. How far is it to Fran Sanshisco again?"

"Four thousand miles, thereabouts." She exploded in a shower of giggles.

"Right! Bedder get on with it then." I reached for my skates, and a midsize backpack containing a poncho, ultra light sleeping bag, bug suit, cook pot, mug, spoon, water bottle, $120 in cash, and a copy of the Atlantic slides for giving talks. "Al, no more booze mate. We're arseholed as it is."

Still squabbling, the entire pub spilled out behind us to where the Pinellas Trail picked up northwards. Using Nancy to brace against, I slipped on my skates, ratcheted down the straps, and shouldered my rucksack. It weighed only thirty-five pounds, but felt like a hundred and thirty-five. It was the first time I'd be carrying it fully laden.

I tried giving Nancy a farewell hug, and nearly tipped over. "Thanks for everything Nance. I'll call you tomorrow morning and let you know how far I've got, okay?"

To roistering yells and wolf whistles, I took my first steps. The wheels rolled forward obligingly.

Okay, I'm off…

Compensating for the extra weight was going to take some getting used to. The skates started to accelerate. My arms started to windmill. My feet suddenly shot out from underneath me like two bars of soap.

THUUNK!

I found myself staring at the sky, sprawling like a beetle. A second later, the *VICTORY!* medal conked me square in the head.

The crowd roared with delight. *"Ooorayyy!"*

Quietly, I swore to myself. *Bugger, shit, fuck, bollocks,* expletives repeated almost mantra-like since leaving Fort Lauderdale.

Just then, a young girl shot past on a pair of roller skates, pink tassels streaming out behind.

"Watch out, she's going to beat you!" someone yelled.

Provoked, I struggled to my feet and set off again. *Right, off we go.... remember to lean forward... Good, that's more like it! Oh... Oh no...*

The skates had a mind of their own, steering off the path. The wheels hit gravel and stopped dead, sending me flying.

"It's gonnae take ye a while tae get there Jason," I heard Al shout, followed by a chorus of raucous laughter.

Two humiliating falls later, I finally made it around the first bend and out of sight of my jeering compatriots. My head reeled with the boozy exertion. A bush under a footbridge appeared.

Perfect spot for a quick snooze...

When I opened my eyes, it was morning.

Slipping on my sandals, I staggered the hundred yards to the phone booth outside the Rose & Crown, and dialled a number.

"Hi Nancy," I croaked into the receiver. "It's Jason." My head was pounding.

"Oh... uh... yes... Hello." The voice on the other end didn't sound too hot, either. "How are things with you? Can't be any worse than me."

"Well, I'm alive. Just thought I'd check in like we agreed."*

"Did you reach highway nineteen yet?"

"Um, not exactly."

DESPITE BEING DISMALLY hung-over, the restoration of a good percentage of motor skills made a world of difference to staying upright. Before

---

* With the hotel office at her disposal, Nancy operated a base camp to monitor our progress across country. Every few days, Steve and I would call in with our positions.

long, I was skimming along at a respectable clip, relishing the smooth surface and absence of traffic.

I came upon an old railroad car set back from the trail, a crude sign overhead advertising "Dino's Toy Shop." Needing a breather, I slipped off my skates and padded over to investigate. Inside was an old man in a blue boiler suit, presumably Dino himself, sculpting Christmas toys on a lathe. Seeing me, he switched off the machine. We talked about Christmas in America, how it differed from England, and his neighbour's dog, Ginger, a bundle of fur lying at my feet.

"He's just a Heinz 57," Dino said affectionately, leaning down to scratch the mutt behind the ears. "Nothin' special. But you know somethin'? He has the best character of any dog I ever met. Mixed breeds always do."

The conversation turned to money, careers, chasing the American Dream. I asked Dino what he, aged nearly eighty, felt really mattered in life.

"Take only what you need," he replied. "And you'll leave the world much like how you found it."

He gave me a tiny alligator carved from wood. When I placed it in the palm of my hand, it waggled its head and tail back and forth.

A good luck charm, I thought, *to see me safely to San Francisco...*

"And remember," the old sage called out as I prepared to skate away. "Life. It's over before you know it."

THE PINELLAS TRAIL ended at Port Richey, a total hole, just one prefabricated roadside shed after another—Dunkin' Donuts, Cash-n-Go Pawn, Fast Cheap Divorce. Forced onto bustling State Highway 19, I began elbowing north with all the other traffic bound for the state capital, Tallahassee.

It was a nightmare. Cars and trucks hurtled by, missing me by inches. A taxi passed on the grass embankment to make a point of being momentarily inconvenienced. Someone lobbed a beer can filled with piss. More often than not, however, "Get off the goddamn road!" was the typical preamble. So typical, in fact, that "Get off the goddamn road you fucking asshole" made for a refreshing change.

At Weeki Wachee, a highway patrol car pulled in front of me, lights flashing. For the umpteenth time that morning, I was told to get off the goddamn road. If I continued, I'd be looking at a $200 fine, more than my entire cross-country budget.

"It's fer your own safety," barked the officer. "If the older folks don't run ya down 'cos they can't see, the rednecks'll do it jus' fer fun. 'Sides, it's illegal to skate on a state highway."

Once he'd pushed off, I sat on the verge and watched the traffic drone past, feeling utterly miserable. The whole business of trying to skate across the US suddenly seemed all too impossible. The near misses and volleys of abuse were one thing, but how long before I was arrested? San Francisco was still more than 4,000 miles away, and playing the dumb tourist card wouldn't last forever. It was only a matter of time before some over-zealous cop ran a background check and discovered I hadn't even cleared US Customs and Immigration.* I'd be summarily deported. Expedition Game Over.

Defeated, I lay down in the grass and began to cry.

WHEN I AWOKE, my ears were filled with the sound of traffic, but my head was clear. I knew what to do. Cradling my skates, I started walking. My bid to skate across country was over. I needed to get back to St Petersburg and pick up a more sensible means of transportation, one I should have chosen from the beginning.

---

* My passport was still in the UK. Thanks to the press cock-up, and America being (as yet) relaxed on border security, we'd slipped into Miami unchallenged.

A bicycle.

I came to a turn-off, the 476 heading east. I took it. Perhaps there was a town with bus service? Walking felt good. But after an hour of tramping, I'd covered only three and a half miles. My arms were aching from carrying the skates. It was already four o'clock, sundown by six.

Sod it, I thought. *There can't be too many cops out here…*

I slipped my skates back on.

It was a quiet country road, super-smooth with hardly any traffic. A sweeping avenue of trees offered respite from the sun, and the few motorists that passed were friendly, waving and giving me a wide berth. Horses leaned over fences, their ears pricked. Organic veggie stands marked the entrance to people's properties, trust jars filled with money.

Over the next hour, I skated thirteen miles to the little town of Brooksville.

Arriving at a T-junction, I stopped to ask directions at the Lake Lindsay Grocery Store, a tatty wood and brick building with a creaking sign promising "America's Coldest Beer." As I sat unbuckling my skates on one of the tree stumps outside, I heard a voice.

"Well ah'll be darned! If it ain't that crazy guy on roller skates we saw back there."

I turned to see two old-timers levering themselves out of a pickup loaded with timber.

"Them ain't roller skates," said the other. "Them's the new thangs the kids are usin' these days, with all the wheels in a row."

The driver introduced himself as Bi-ill with two syllables. Beehill was barrel-chested, his dungarees rolled halfway up to his knees. "So where ya headed?" He grinned and summoned a gobbet of inky-black saliva from the back of his throat, landing it expertly between his hobnail boots.

For explanation, I fished out the world map I carried in my rucksack, and unfolded it on the gravel. A small crowd from the store gathered as I began tracing the circumnavigation route.

"Ida done the same thing at yer age," said Beehill, discharging another thick squirt of tobacco.

"Thas right!" cried his buddy, George. "Worst thing a man can do is abide by the rules. Like that damned fool gov'ment o' ours in Washington. If they had it their way, we'd awl be bled dry payin' their taxes an' followin' dumb-ass reg'lations!"

It was fighting talk from a pair of misty-eyed old Confederates, dreaming of what might have been. For deep in their rebel hearts burned a flickering flame, that one fine day The South would rise again.

Until that day came, the old warhorses had to console themselves with dredging up gloriously embroidered stories of their youth. As the audience grew, they reverted to their former nineteen-year-old selves. "When we wuz outlaws!" hooted George.

Beehill boasted how he'd once nailed the local tax inspector inside his own outhouse. "Used six-inch nails through the doorframe." He slapped the air. "That gov'ment bastard weren't niver gittin' out!"

The women chuckled and rolled their eyes.

At the same time I regaled twelve-year-old Adam with some of our Atlantic tales. A faraway look stole across his face as he pored over the map.

"So, yer skatin' all the way to *San Francisco?*" His eyes widened to the size of dinner plates.

"Well, not any more." And I told him how I'd given up on the idea, and was heading back to St Pete.

The boy looked scandalized. "Whadya mean, yer quit'n? Why?"

I sighed. "It's too hard, what with all the traffic and the polic—"

"But ya cain't!" Adam interrupted. "You 'n Steve awready crossed the Atlan'ic. If ya can do that, ya can do anythang!"

That last line slapped me across the face. It was the same one that echoed off the walls of the classrooms we gave presentations to. "Whether it's pedalling across an ocean," we told the kids, "or wanting to be a basketball player, a vet, a nurse, or an actor. If you have a dream, never, ever give up, okay? You can do anything."

Adam was right. I was being a pussy. You *can* do anything. You just have to believe in yourself enough. Thanking the boy for his inspirational kick up the backside, I strapped on my skates, waved goodbye to Beehill and George, and hit County Road 41 heading north. Valuable time had been lost, and a renewed sense of purpose lent urgency to my stride.

I had a goddamn country to skate across after all.

Brute conviction isn't always enough. Sometimes you have to think laterally, use Critical Eye, and adapt. I laughed aloud as my skate wheels hummed on the blacktop. *What the hell were you thinking skating on the main highway?* I should have been looking for smaller roads with less traffic and fewer cops, but still big enough to have a smooth, level surface. So what if they weren't as direct? As long as they were heading roughly northwest, the "C" roads would be infinitely more enjoyable. That alone made the time pass quicker, and the distance seem shorter.

Two days later, I stumbled upon the Withlacoochee Trail, a reclaimed railroad nosing through the languid swamps of central Florida. Its sinuous name alone suggested a seductive alternative to even the most isolated county road. Spanish moss dangled like wizards' beards from the overhanging branches, and crickets chafed in the dense vegetation bordering the narrow path.

Being up and skating by sunrise was now key to beating the heat. Even then I'd be cooked by midday and needing to rest up for the afternoon, replenishing body fluids. Only towards evening would the throttling heat slacken enough to continue, which often meant skating until dark to achieve my daily target of thirty-five miles. The challenge was then to find a suitable stand of saplings to string my poncho between, providing some element of shelter from the rainstorms that struck during the night.

A few joggers and hikers passed me on the trail, and a cyclist named Jack who was also crossing the country, but from west to east. We stopped and chatted. Before riding away, he handed me his spare can of pepper spray. "For the dogs and the weirdos," he said.

Other dangers lurked in the bayous. Waking at dawn on the edge of Tsala Apopka Lake, I slipped naked into the limpid green water, its mirrored surface simmering with light tendrils of steam. As I floated on my back, gazing dreamily at the sky, a pair of eyeballs popped up beside me.

When I'd enquired about alligators in Lee's Coffee Shop a few days earlier, Robert Zimgg assured me there was nothing to worry about. "If you're in the water and see a gator, just pretend you're one too and swim underwater at it."

At the time, surrounded by coffee-slurping patrons and a cappuccino machine gurgling away in the background, his advice had sounded plausible. But now that I was actually sharing the same bathwater with one, intentionally going closer to something that should have died millions of years ago along with the rest of the dinosaurs, struck me as foolhardy in the extreme. Even with a brain the size of an acorn, could alligators be so dumb as to mistake a human for one of their own?

I swam slowly away instead, trying not to splash or appear panicked. The reptile followed at a distance, more intrigued than anything, probably wondering what this strange albino creature, clearly unsuited to water, was doing floundering around in its backyard.

July 23. 11:45 am

"AH'M AWRIGHT! 'Cos the Good Lawd woke me up this mornin'."

I was sitting inside the Dixie Country Store, ten miles west of Talla-hassee, waiting out the heat. A posse of older black men was discussing politics, the Good Book, and luxuriating in the fact that, "The Good Lawd decided to grant me another day, yes siree!"

This was now the Deep South, land of swamps, cow pastures, eu-calyptus trees, and god-fearing men and women, both black and white, who lived side-by-side like keys on a piano, but seldom in harmony it seemed.

"Mah nigger rang this morning for a ride," a white customer had voiced to his circle of cronies earlier. "But he was drunk, so I told 'im to call t'morra."

They turned to stare at me, waiting for a reaction—they'd spotted my long hair when I first walked in. I pretended not to hear, and con-tinued writing up my journal. The old boy tried again, launching into a diatribe about Greenpeace. "An' if the envir'ment gits polluted, then tha's the way its gotta be, 'cos America *needs* the steel don' it?"

Grunting their approval, the rednecks looked at me again. One of them gestured to the skates under my chair. "So where ya headed on them there thangs?"

I looked up from my scribbling. "Montgomery, Alabama. Oklaho-ma. Kansas. San Francisco eventually."

This didn't faze him one bit. "So you'll be out with the darkies tonight then won't ya!" And he leered at me with a mouthful of foul, broken teeth while his buddies hacked and hawed with glee, hammer-ing their fists on the table.

When they weren't lobbing insults or cans of piss, white drivers in the South were largely indifferent to the sight of someone rollerblading down the highway. In comparison, African Americans became animat-ed. Some waved as they passed. Others shook their heads and smiled, teeth gleaming. "Where ya headed?" they'd shout out the window. Or just mouth the words, "Sweet Jesus! On *rowllerblades…*"

Not all were friendly. In Gretna, I was resting near a house painted a poisonous green when the owner, an obese black man, got in his gas guzzler, drove the hundred yards to where I was sitting, and told me to "Git goin'!"

I told him I wasn't going anywhere. I was hot and bothered and on public property.

The man made a face and promptly drove the hundred yards back to his house. Then his wife stuck her head out the front door and started screeching. All I could make out was, *"Git oan widya!"* and *"Homliss gudfa nuthin'!"*

Five miles beyond Chattahoochee, I turned north towards Dothan, leaving Lake Seminole to the east. A predictable bullet-ridden sign marked the Alabama state line. The bayous gave way to farmland, rolling fields of low-lying peanuts and cotton shrubs fringed by soaring stands of timber. Now at seven hundred miles into the journey, I was skating entire days without falling, and getting the hang of braking with a "t-stop." This involved dragging the right boot behind the left at ninety degrees, more efficient than using the rubber heel stoppers. Even so, when the fully laden logging trucks thundered past, I had to lean back at the critical moment to avoid being bowled over by the backdraught.

The only way to reach the kids' summer camp at Wetumpka where I was due to give a presentation was to take US Route 231, a major thoroughfare. Intimidated by the volume of traffic and lack of hard shoulder, I experimented with skating at night. The road was virtually empty after midnight, and the high beams of vehicles gave plenty of forewarning to get off the road. It was also a lot cooler. The only downside was the road kill. Several times since leaving Fort Lauderdale, skating in the pre-dawn gloom, I'd hit a decomposing armadillo at full tilt. So, before setting out from Troy to Montgomery, a night skate of some fifty miles, I stopped at a hardware store and bought a flashlight.

It would be my farthest skate yet, taking all night to reach We-tumpka by eleven the next morning. Maintaining sufficient energy was paramount. Most evenings I'd simply pull off the road, gather some kindling, and boil up some rice in my cooking pot, a can of sardines thrown in completing a meal. Tonight I didn't have time.

Shortly after nine, a neon sign heralded "Ed's Diner   GRAND OPENING." Without bothering to take off my skates, I leaned through the open doorway. A song by Confederate Railroad was twanging on the radio, the vocalist expressing his undying love for *women just a little on the trashy side*…

"Do you have any meals for under three bucks?" I asked the wait-ress.

She looked up from clearing tables. "Oh, ah'm sorry, hon. Kitchen's just clowsed."

"Never mind." As I turned to totter back into the night, an ageing biker at the bar growled at me. "Where ya headed?"

This was Tom, it turned out, owner of a greying ponytail and the battered Kawasaki parked outside. I told him about the expedition, the staff listening in. Next thing a burger and fries magically appeared, and Ed the proprietor was on the phone to the local radio station.

The song ended, and the voice of the DJ came booming over the speakers with an all stations advisory for truckers. *"Now ah'll be the first to admit that ah've seen some pretty strange thangs in mah time, but y'all hear this. There's this Bridish guy rollerbladin' up Route two thirty one from Ed's Diner to Montgomery—in the Lord's name, I know not what for. But fer all ya eighteen-wheelers out there, y'all be careful. Don't go runnin' the stoopid sonofabitch over now. They need 'im up at Camp Chandler fer a preezentation to the kids t'morra, and they need 'im ALIVE!"*

Ed and the two servers, Linda and Janet, started whooping like coyotes. Tom said the GRAND OPENING sign had been up well over a month, but the diner was still struggling to put bums on seats. This was the most advertising they'd had in weeks.

On cue, an eighteen-wheeler pulled into the parking lot.

"Bringin' em in awready!" hollered Ed, punching the air.

A fat-bellied thug of a trucker complete with handlebar moustache appeared in the doorway.

"Where's that crazy mother-fuckin' rollerblader?" he thundered. "'Cos ah'm gonna run his Limey ass down!"

"Aww, c'moan Rusty," cooed Linda, throwing an arm around the trucker's hairy shoulders. "Why don't you give the guy a doh-nation?" She winked at me. "Ol' Rusty's bark is worse than his bite. Yer jus' a big teddy bear now ainchya Rusty." And the trucker chuckled as she tweaked his whiskers playfully.

"Ah ain't payin' for nobody to commit su'cide," snorted Rusty. But he flung a five-dollar bill across the bar at me anyway.

By CLOSING TIME, the traffic had slacked off enough to continue. Tom offered to escort me on his motorcycle, but I declined. He'd had a skinful of tequila, I reminded him, and the highway was bestrewn with enough road kill as it was.

The surface was good and smooth, and my torch lit up the scattered carcasses well enough to maintain a steady pace. The problem was boredom. With nothing to look at save the dancing yellow beam, I took to counting the mile markers to stay awake. When I did at one point drift off and veer into the middle of the road, a blast from an oncoming car brought me to my senses, and back to the edge.

After four hours of non-stop skating, my calf muscles were twitching with fatigue, and the tendons in my left foot beginning to strain. I longed to take a break. But the Montgomery orbital road was still ten miles away. I needed to keep going to miss rush hour traffic.

It was on a downhill stretch that I heard the snarling airbrakes of a semi-trailer close behind. Going too fast to stop, I tucked my knees like a downhill skier to give the driver more time to overtake. Another truck suddenly appeared, coming from the opposite direction. My brain did the calculation in an instant: we'd be passing the same point in the road together.

Both drivers opened up with their air horns, and switched to full beam, lighting up the surrounding trees in elaborate detail. The thundering wheels and squealing brakes became a deafening roar. At the last second—night turning to day in the glare of the halogens, glint of steel fenders slashing across my retinas—I dove. A wall of air slammed me broadside as the trucks blew past, spinning my body like a rag doll and hurling me into a tangle of thorns.

I lay there for several minutes, waiting for the adrenaline surge to subside, thinking of what the old-timer near Lake Okeechobee had said. *They'll run ya down, see. They'll jus… run ya down…*

ONCE OR TWICE since setting out from the coast, I'd wondered whether rollerblading through The South was really such a good idea, especially with long hair and earrings. After all, Peter Fonda and Dennis Hopper had fallen foul of hippy-hating rednecks in *Easy Rider*. But that was just fiction, I told myself. Now that I was actually on the road, I hadn't felt seriously threatened. Yet.

But what if I were black, or of some ethnicity other than Caucasian? How long before a gun-toting good ol' boy took a potshot at me then?

The truth, as I was starting to discover, is that prejudice doesn't follow any preset lines, either south of the thirty-sixth parallel in the US, or anywhere else in the world. Fearsome-looking rednecks became my new best friend once they saw past the earrings: "At first we thought you was a goddamn faggot, but yer awright." Pious Christians turned chary at the sight of my tattoos, apprehensive their sanctimonious doorsteps might be sullied by inviting me into their homes. And in spite of the smiles, not a single African American chose to cross the colour divide and be the first to strike up a conversation.

No, I wrote in my journal, *prejudice is just another word for fear. Fear of anything different. Fear of anyone threatening a person's set of deeply enshrined beliefs, habits, ideas, or opinions central to their sense of identity and place in the world...*

In short, memetic tribalism. The South's only difference was being a land that time forgot, passed over by the shifting sentiments of an evermore politically correct, liability-conscious world. A world in which people learn to keep their mouths shut and prejudices hidden if they want to get along in life—just more fear-induced behaviour modification.

Individual exceptions abounded, of course. Skating through the town of Coosada one evening, I passed a family barbecuing in their front yard.

"Looks like someone could do with a beer!" hollered a bald, middle-aged man holding up a can of Bud Light. The late afternoon air was wet and sticky like molten molasses, and I was sweltering from the day's skate. When a sandy-haired woman offered something to eat, I gratefully accepted. My appetite was raging.

None of them showed the slightest interest in how I looked or what I was doing. As far as they were concerned, I was just someone breezing through from A to B. If I had a reason for using inline skates as opposed to a car or a bicycle, they never asked. They were unsophisticated, unpresumptuous, genuine, and sincere, uncontaminated by fabricated frills or social graces.

In a few days, the whole family was moving to Colorado in a U-Haul van, the wife told me.

"Why?" I asked.

She was sitting in a lawn chair, two small children fighting in her lap. "We jus' felt like it, I guess." She shrugged. "Only decided yesterday. Mah husband builds houses, so we're gonna find another small town and start again. We'll get by."

THREE NIGHTS LATER, I reached Aliceville, Alabama. It was past ten by the time I rolled into town. Almost immediately, I ran into the town sheriff. The difference between the overbearing highway patrol officers and their more congenial local law enforcement counterparts was already clear to me. The sheriff offered to put me up in a motel—a kind gesture, but I refused nonetheless.

Instead, I slept under an ornamental tree on the lawn of one of the ubiquitous Baptist churches. When it began to rain, I squeezed under the porch overhang. In the morning, I awoke with a start to a dark figure standing over me.

"You're trespassing," said the pastor. He wore a white dog collar and black jeans and his hands were planted on his hips.

"I am?" I mumbled, rubbing my eyes to better bring the apparition into focus.

"I got a congregation turnin' up here for early service. You better git goin', else I'll have to call the sheriff."

Obviously, he'd never preached the Good Samaritan sermon. Still cocooned in my sleeping bag, I shifted to a sitting position to better face my adversary.

"Well, I wish you would," I replied, looking to take the wind out of his sails. "Then I can thank him again for his Christian offer to put me up in a motel last night."

Either the gibe went over the preacher's head, or he chose to ignore it; he continued to nag.

"Fuck this," I muttered. It was too early for a pissing contest. Slipping on my skates and stuffing the sleeping bag in my backpack, I beat a hasty retreat.

Evangelicals one. Infidel zero.

Later, after slogging along a particularly miserable stretch of "band-aid" surface—gravel chips sprinkled on a tar base—that chewed my skate wheels to bits, I lay down under a magnificent shade tree to catch my breath. I was starting to nod off when a shiny black Buick pulled up. In the front were two old bats giving me daggers.

"You can't stay there," croaked the driver. She had the po-faced expression of a vulture, and her bony hands gripped the steering wheel like claws. "You'll have to move on."

"I'm just resting out of the heat," I said.

"We don't care," squawked the other, looking equally cadaverous. "That's private property you're on."

I was on the recently mowed drainage ditch. "This is part of the highway," I countered.

"No it ain't." Her reddish hair was permed at the front like a rooster's comb. "It's church property."

It was then that I noticed the Baptist church behind me.

Oh god, I thought, *here we go again...* I'd had some coffee. I was ready for combat.

"Are you both true believers?" I asked, changing tack.

The battle-axe in the passenger seat glared at me, her eyes narrowing to slits. "What's that got to do with anything?"

"What if I told you I was Jesus of Nazareth needing to rest by the side of the road?"

They digested what I'd said. "We wouldn't believe you!" the driver finally exclaimed.

"Why not?"

"'Cos you're nothing but a bum!"

"Jesus was a bum, tramping around Galilee with just the shirt on his back."

Both of them were trembling now, their topknots quivering with rage. "How *dare* you!" gasped the passenger. "You're an evil man mister, a blasphemer, takin' the Good Lord's name in vain."

"Actually, you're right on both counts," I admitted. "I'm not Jesus. And I am a bum."

With that I stood up and turned around, yanked down my shorts, and bared my arse at them.

I heard two sharp intakes of breath.

Delivered of this infantile yet supremely satisfying gesture, I sat down again. Wheels spun. Gravel flew. Only two words made it through the billowing shards of dust and grit: "sheriff" and "arrested."

What was it with these self-righteous Bible Thumpers, I wondered? Every time their faith was challenged, they ran to the sheriff like teacher's pet.

ROAD KILL MENU OUTSIDE THE COCHRANE CAFÉ

"Eating food is more fun when you know it's been hit on the run."
- Flat Cat (single or in a stack) $2.95
- Chicken (that didn't cross the road) $3.95
- Rigor Mortis Tortoise $6.75

If you can guess what it is, you eat for free.

August 3

Long skate up from Macon towards Louisville ... road surface terrible for the first 5 miles ... legs very tired and feet sore ... push on ... hills start ... running low on water and getting dark ... monster hill done in 2 x stages ... ask kids playing outside a farmhouse for water ... dad comes out and offers a beer... Kids get their

own rollerblades on and skate alongside for a few hundred yards… Skate on without
lights … 8 miles to Louisville … stop at county store for tin of luncheon meat and
bread. Very tired now … fall heavily on the way out … decide to sleep in the woods
rather than risk getting nailed on the road.

Had running battles with ants all night … they went crazy over the luncheon
meat … just kept on coming and coming on all sides. Then these huge black ants
appeared out of the undergrowth. All they wanted to do was lick me with their hairy
tongues—for the salt and moisture, I suppose… (Journal)

THE WIND SPEED increased during the night. By daylight, the tops of the
trees were heaving to and fro. I rolled effortlessly into Louisville mid-
morning, literally blown the six miles with the wind at my back.

Taking temporary shelter in a store on Main Street, I learned of a
hurricane crossing the Gulf Coast at Pensacola, a hundred and twenty
miles to the south. It was heading due north according to the owner,
who offered to call a local motel to see if they had any vacancies. When
I told him my budget didn't stretch to such extravagances, he offered to
put me up in his own home until the storm passed.

He gave me a hand-drawn map and a set of keys to get in.

The front door yielded with a creak, the shadows inside recoiling.
A sudden chill washed through me. There was something unnerving
about the loose floorboards, and the way the wind seemed to whisper
secrets through the cracks in the bare walls, as if happiness had packed
up its bags and left long ago.

Verne arrived a few hours later and showed me to a room in the
basement where I could sleep. It was spartan, a bare mattress and the
window boarded and framed with cobwebs.

Outside, Hurricane Erin began to flex her muscles, snapping off
tree branches and flinging them across the garden. A visceral moan
was coming from the power lines that flailed against a sky filled almost
entirely by a gigantic slab of dark cloud, layered as if sculpted on a
potter's wheel.

Then darkness came.

"I'm just a *simple* man, see." My host spoke slowly and deliberately, heavy creases curving down around the edges of his mouth. "Not very able."

We were sitting at the kitchen table, talking. Or, in my case, listening. The timbers creaked and a lone light bulb flickered.

"Nonsense Verne!" I laughed nervously the morbid atmosphere was spooking me. "You're as capable as the next man."

But he wasn't listening. "I wanted to talk with you some more, see. You have an education, from the University of London." He stopped and fixed me with his sallow, watery eyes. "Educated people are *better* people, see."

"How so?"

"A person with an education has morals."

"Says who?"

"Mother."

I shook my head. "What about Hilter, Machiavelli, Stalin, they were all educa—"

Verne was rambling now about sexual deviances, of which he said he didn't approve, and Winston Churchill, of whom he did. "He was an *educated* man, see…"

Later, lying in the basement, my mind began racing. There was something unsettling about Verne's soft-spoken manner, and the way he looked at me with those damp, empty eyes. I couldn't sleep. I was afraid if I did, I might never wake up.

America is full of crazy loners, I thought wildly. *Billy No Mates like Jeffery Dahmer and Ed Gein yammering to their dead mothers. What if I end up buried under a rose bush in the garden with my dick in the freezer? I haven't phoned Nancy in over a week. People wouldn't even know where to start looking…*

At first light, coward that I am, I crept out of the house, leaving a hastily scribbled note on the kitchen table.

The wind was gusting still, whipping the trees. Giant raindrops drummed out a tattoo on the pavement. We'd been lucky. The eye of the storm had passed to the west. Unable to skate on a wet road strewn with debris, I started walking along the railway track towards Ackerman.

By early afternoon, the rain had stopped, the wind died, and the sun even showed signs of coming out. Life resonated once more in the burgeoning greenness bordering the railroad. My ears rang with the sound of croaking frogs, chirruping crickets, and all the reverberations of a primeval swamp that hadn't changed much in three billion years. I felt guilty bailing without saying goodbye. My host had been a bit weird, yes, but kind nonetheless, and I'd reciprocated his Southern hospitality with paranoia.

Then again, I reminded myself, *travelling alone is like that. You have to trust your gut...*

I kept walking, and for the first time since arriving in the US caught sight of animals that weren't just doormats on the road. Deer grazed in the dappled shadows, and a beaver swimming across a lake slapped its tail in warning at my approach. Between the man-made ridges of steel, however, there was only death: the skeleton of a dog still attached by its collar to a coupling, victim of sadistic human cruelty; and every few hundred yards the remains of a tortoise marked by an empty shell.

A dusky kid dawdling in the opposite direction explained how the unfortunate critters took an ill-fated turn at level crossings. Then they became trapped, he said, unable to climb over or under the rails.

"They'z jus' keep walkin' 'n walkin' tils they die o' thirst. Or git ate."

What a way to go, I thought. *Staggering along a railway track with your tongue hanging out, blood slowly boiling to a hundred degrees...*

And it got me thinking about life, and about death, and about the thin line between the two. And how sometimes you have a choice, and how other times you don't. And how the line is sometimes so thin you can barely make it out, and you end up taking a wild leap of faith anyway.

IT WAS THREE in the morning when the fire ants struck. Bright orange and deceptively small for the amount of suffering they inflict, fire ants work as a team, crawling undetected onto their prey before biting en masse for maximum potency. Ever since my *Buzz Off!* suit disintegrated a week previously, I'd been dousing myself with bug repellent before going to sleep. On this occasion, however, being the sneaky little bastards they are, they didn't attack just anywhere. *No siree!* They chose the one part of my anatomy they knew I couldn't apply diethyltoluamide to without putting myself in the hospital.

My willy.

By morning, the inflammation was so bad I could barely skate. Limping into Winona, I first hit the post office to pick up a set of replacement skate wheels sent by my wheel sponsor, Cyko. The second priority was to resolve the dreadful chaffing. A thrift store out by the interstate looked promising, but when I asked the old dear behind the counter if she had any loose-fitting shorts, she shook her head.

"I only gat these here shorts fer women," she replied, shambling over to a rack and picking out a knee-length skirt covered in red and white checks. "They's called culottes."

The price was seventy-five cents. *What the hell,* I thought. *As long as I can skate in them, who cares what they look like?*

In the end, of course, everyone cared. At the time, I just paid the money, slipped them on, and got on my way. The relief was instantaneous, like night and day to the tight Lycra. A steady flow of air wafted up one leg and down the other, having a blissful cooling effect on my swollen member. Fellow road-users seemed equally impressed.

Cars tooted as they passed, and truckers approaching from behind wolf-whistled from their windows. That is until they drew level and clocked the goatee and duct tape over my nipples to prevent sunburn, then their jaws dropped.

And this was just the beginning. On the road to Grenada, I heard the whoop of a siren and turned to see a patrol car pulling over. Out stepped a six-and-a-half-foot tall state trooper with a bull neck. Slipping on his wide-brimmed hat, he marched towards me.

"Someone called in. Sump'm 'bout a cross-dressin' hippy skatin' on the highway."

"Well, if I see one, officer," I replied cheerfully. "You'll be the first to know."

He stared at me in disbelief. "Just what, in tarnation, d'ya think ya doin' boy? Skatin' on the highway is against the law! You bin drinkin'?"*

"No sir."

"Then what's with the…" He waved at the culottes.

"Well, last night I got bitten by fire ants on my, um"—I leaned forward to whisper it—"*Johnson.*"

The officer flinched. "Step into the car son. Ah'm 'onna have to take ya in for a li'l grillin'."

Sitting in the back seat, I started to feel uneasy. Had he said grillin' or drillin'? And why did that film keep looping in my head? The one where a weekend hunter gets wheel barrowed around a log cabin in the Appalachians by a pair of sex-starved hillbillies before being made to squeal like a pig.

I realized I was being watched in the rear view mirror. And was that a smirk on the officer's face?

"Where ya from son?"

---

*   The ruling on inline skating in 1995 varied from state to state and county to county. In some areas, it was considered illegal. Other jurisdictions classified skaters as pedestrians.

"England."

"En–ger–land." He mouthed the syllables. "So, is this some kind o' cultural thang ya got goin' on here? I mean, do guys over yonder git dressed up in women's clothin' and go… skatin' round the country for shits 'n giggles or somethin'?"

I didn't dare mention my Johnson again, in case he got the wrong idea. Instead, I wracked my brain for old English traditions. Morris dancing, nettle eating, and sheep worrying sprang readily to mind, but none of these came close to explaining rollerblading through Mississippi in a skirt.

Now the Scots on the other hand…

"You could say it's cultural," I replied. "In Scotland they call this a kilt."

The officer raised his eyebrows. "Scot–land ya say? Well 'arl be darned. My great granddaddy came from Scot–land."

"Oh yeah?"

"So is Scot–land near to Eng–er–land?"

"Right next door."

"Is that so? And y'all eat that stuff made out of… brains and saw-dust—wha's it called again?"

"Haggis."

"Yeah, that's it. Mah wife made it once." He laughed. "Tasted like two-week-ol' Georgia road kill!"

I, too, laughed, if only to fan the embryonic spark between us. Before long, we were on to tepid beer, Margaret Thatcher, sponge cakes, and cricket.

We came to a pedestrian crossing in the centre of town. A woman and her young child peered in to see who was being arrested.

The state trooper turned to me. "Ah hayul Jason. Ah can't take ya to the station. Yer gonna be humiliated. 'Sides, I feel like you and me is kinfolk now. From the motherland, right?"

I smiled feebly and nodded. Apart from the likelihood of co-starring in the prison version of *Deliverance*, I'd undoubtedly undergo a background check. It wouldn't take long for the police department to discover I was in the country illegally.

"Ah'm 'onna git me a kilt like that," the officer was saying, eyeing my culottes longingly. "Reconnect with mah roots."

While I wrestled with the image of the 250-pound state trooper in a red and white chequered skirt, he made a U-turn, and drove me back to where he'd picked me up. As I retrieved my gear from the back seat, he rolled down his window and waved a ten-dollar bill at me.

"Jeet yet?" he said.

"I'm sorry?"

"I said, *jeet* yet?" He jabbed a finger at his mouth.

"Uh, yes. I ate earlier, thanks."

He thrust the note into my hand. "Well take this anyhow. Gitcha a real meal and put some meat on that skinny li'l ass, 'cos y'ain't never passin' for a Suthern gal lookin' like that. Git some shorts, too. Keep them fire ants outta ya Limey pants."

FIVE MILES LATER, nearing the junction at Grenada, something fluttered out of the window of a passing station wagon. It was a pair of red basketball shorts with a handwritten note inside one of the pockets. "You need these!" It read.

No shit, I thought.

Had the officer sent them ahead? There was no way of knowing. One thing was for certain, though. I could finally get those horny truckers off my back.

I CROSSED THE mighty Mississippi River late in the afternoon of Friday August 11. Almost immediately, there was a shift in ambience. You could almost smell the money, paunchy white corporate types riding around on lawn tractors while the black inhabitants of the Helena Projects bobbed and skulked behind chain-link fences. Technically, Arkansas was still The South. In reality, it was a world away from the idiosyncratic states of Mississippi and Alabama I'd left behind.

Not without incident, though.

Earlier, on the east side of the bridge, a red Pontiac had pulled in front of me. The driver side window slid down, and a can of Budweiser emerged, dangling from crimson-tipped fingers. In the wing mirror, a pair of sunglasses studied my approach.

"Gol–lee," said a low, sexy voice as I came alongside. "Hot, ain't it?" The driver, a stunning brunette, dipped her shades, looked me up and down, and levelled her liquid brown eyes at mine. "Wah don't ya c'moan and sit in the back? Drink a beer with us."

Another beauty sprawled in the passenger seat, her legs crossed, mouth curled enticingly. My heart missed a beat.

"I should… really be getting on," I stammered. "Cross the river before it gets dar—"

"Oh c'moan."

Well, maybe there's time for a quick one…

Slipping off my skates, I got in the back seat.

"We saw ya back there in Lula. Thought ya might like to come back to our place for a li'l fun."

The girls dissolved into peals of dirty giggles.

My blood began thumping. I hadn't been with a woman in—how long? A threesome might put me over the edge.

They were no-nonsense, down-to-earth Southern girls, born and raised in Mississippi. Janelle worked in a hair salon, Mary Ann as a croupier on the "Lady Luck" casino boat moored on the river.

The chat went back and forth, and they giggled some more. Janelle handed me another beer. "Gol–lee," she purred seductively, "ya sure got a cute accent."

I said I begged to differ. Their voices were utterly captivating, words slithering off moistened tongues and dripping from perfectly painted lips, pouring like honey-dew-lullaby-drops into my ears and sending me into a trance. The way Janelle kept saying Gol–lee…

"So, ya wanna come back and have some fun?"

More provocative laughter. But something had slipped out of sync, like the picture and sound on a TV set. Mary Ann was talking, Janelle laughing, their mouths moving in slow motion, voices garbled as if we were all underwater. The high-pitched shrill of the crickets kept getting louder. The scarlet plush of the seat kept sinking deeper. I was drenched in sweat, ears throbbing. The inside of the car started to spin.

When I heard the engine start, I couldn't move. My legs and arms felt bound by invisible cords. I couldn't speak either. My face was frozen. *Did they put something in my beer?* Only my eyes continued to function, passive witnesses to events beyond my control.

A rising tide of panic welled up. I needed to get out.

Wooooh—Hooooo— Wooooh—Hooooo—

The booming chant of a freight train cut the spell like a knife, snapping me to my senses.

"I'm sorry… I have to…"—I was clawing frantically for the door handle—"I have to go now." Finding the clasp, I shouldered the door and fell out on the road, dragging my skates and backpack after me.

Two Union Pacific locomotives lumbered into view, hauling boxcar after clattering boxcar westwards.

"Gol-lee. Where ya goin' sweetie?" Janelle called after me. "We was all fixin' to have a good time!"

The fresh air dried the sweat from my face and cleared my head. Still feeling unsteady on my feet, I carried my skates and stumbled towards the bridge. When I looked back, the girls' expressions had changed. Their eyes, no longer filled with longing, were cruel and mocking, and their mouths twisted and jeering. Even their laughter sounded barbed and derisive, until it faded to nothing.

I WAS NOW a third of the way across the country, and my skating coming along in leaps and bounds. Fifty-mile days weren't uncommon, and I hadn't fallen in over a week. I'd also mastered glancing over my left shoulder to monitor vehicles coming up behind without veering inadvertently into their path. A bright orange flag I'd found by the roadside flew from my backpack on a long white cane, lessening my chances of ending up as "the special" on a road kill menu.

In truth, however, the local varmints gave me the biggest run for my money—what little I had left.

Camping on the banks of the White River one evening, clouds of mosquitoes descended at dusk. Out of insect repellent, I lit a fire in one of the designated fire pits, hoping the smoke would act as a deterrent. The bloodthirsty insects took not the slightest bit of notice. As a last resort, I tried covering my arms, legs, neck and head with ash. It made no difference.

Accepting defeat, I washed off in the river. There, fully submerged, I found relief at last. Although beginning their miserable little lives in water, mosquitoes can't swim. For the next forty minutes until it was fully dark and the worst of the infestation over, I lay in the shallows, breathing through the tube of my ballpoint pen. Cheated out of their meal, the mozzies zinged in furious circles inches above my face.

Dogs were another story.

Since Florida, I'd attracted the attention of nearly every living mongrel in the southeast lower 48, it seemed. Alerted by some underground

Canine Bush Telegraph, four-foots of all descriptions came bounding out from every yard, alley, and driveway. My strategy against being bitten was crude but effective. If any of the brutes looked close to taking a mouthful, I unsheathed the umbrella I kept strapped to my backpack, and used the business end as a bayonet.

But skating down a hill in Muldrow, Oklahoma, I met my match.

Three vicious Rhodesian Ridgebacks emerged from an alleyway and tore down the road after me, barking and snarling. They worked as a team, two acting as decoys, the third coming in from behind, aiming for my calves. I reached for my umbrella, but it was gone.

Shit!

Then I remembered. Only that morning I'd ditched it to save weight, the afternoon pattern of monsoonal downpours having petered out after Little Rock.

Frantically, I fumbled in a side pocket for the can of pepper spray. Slipping off the safety, I aimed it behind me, and squeezed the trigger.

Phhhrrrt—

Empty.

Cursing in frustration, I hurled the canister at the dog to my right. It missed by a mile, sailing harmlessly into the bushes beyond.

The one behind me then lunged. By chance, I happened to lift my right foot at the same moment. Powerful jaws locked onto the wheels. Now I was skating along on one foot, at speed, a large furry beast attached to the other. Its accomplices, meanwhile roused by the hunt, snapped and bayed all the more.

Alerted by the ruckus, an old-timer walking up the road began hurling rocks, driving the two off with a few well-aimed throws. At the same time I was losing balance, my arms windmilling. I planted my foot down hard. There was a yelp. Then I was away, gliding free.

AFTER THE SINUOUS C roads of The South, I was looking forward to making better mileage on the long, straight roads of Oklahoma and Kansas, the same magical Land of Oz I remembered with childhood fondness from the famed movie. But after two days of disappointing progress, I was beginning to think The Wizard was right. Kansas was, indeed, an impossible place to get to (or, in Dorothy's case, back to), presumably because the Yellow Brick Road was in such a bloody awful state of disrepair. Blessed at some point in the distant past with a gloriously smooth finish, now it was little more than an obstacle course of gaping cracks and teetering subsidence, requiring the mustering of early playground skills—hopping, skipping, jumping—to negotiate on skates. There was a noticeable lack of munchkins and flying monkeys, too.

Skating through the town of Okemah, a brown pickup drew level. The driver, an unshaven weasel in a baseball cap, glowered at me with glazed, heavy-lidded eyes. He was drunk.

"*Fuggin'asshole,*" he bawled. "*Getowdadafuggin'roadyoufuggin'asshole.*"

If I'd been smarter, I would have reminded myself that it was late on a Friday, payday, in a "wet" county where alcohol was freely available, and a good portion of the male population could elucidate from personal experience the close correlation between alcohol abuse and the inside of a prison cell. And I would have ignored him. But no, my temper flared and my tongue started flapping before my brain could throw the master switch.

"Go fuck yourself," I replied.

This was all the excuse Angry-Redneck-With-Small-Penis needed. He swung the wheel to pin me against the crash barrier. Being triple-lane, the road was wide enough to swerve out of harm's way. I slipped behind the tailgate, crossed the road, and entered a hospital parking lot. Sitting on a grassy mound were three Indian men sharing a bottle concealed in a brown paper bag.

Even if they're wasted, I thought, *as witnesses they're better than nothing...*

I smiled, said hello, and sat down beside them.

The pickup reappeared, the driver looking more belligerent than ever. Gunning his engine, he started doing laps around us, fishtailing the truck wildly—tyres squealing, smoke billowing—cursing me at the top of his voice. He wrestled the wheel one-handed, keeping the other hidden.

After a dozen laps, the angry drunk was still no closer to avenging the five whole seconds he'd lost waiting for a gap in traffic to go around me. With a final screeching doughnut and *"You fuggin'asshole!"* he roared off in a cloud of burning rubber. The truck slowed as it came to the main road. Then I saw something through the rear cab window that sent a chill through me: a hand reaching over to the glove box and tossing a revolver back inside.

Sometimes I forgot. This wasn't sleepy little old England.

IN OKLAHOMA CITY it was stinking hot: 112 degrees with ninety-seven per cent humidity. After picking up the latest set of skate wheels from the post office, I found a pay phone and called Nancy. Steve and Eilbhe were still in New Orleans, apparently, which meant I wasn't falling too far behind. They'd be there a week giving talks and raising funds, before pressing on to East Texas, continuing their southerly track across the country.

Another package was waiting for me, Nancy said, but all the way across town at the Fed Ex depot. It took the rest of the afternoon to get there, an inestimable embuggerance in the heat and the traffic. Yet, I knew my life might depend upon its contents: a revolutionary new parachute system to control my descent off the high mountain passes of the Colorado Rockies and California Sierra Nevada.

At the top of the first hill west of town, I gave it a test run. Tightening the harness around my upper body, I clipped in the karabiner leading to the chute, and pushed off. The gossamer-thin fabric billowed out encouragingly, reducing my speed immediately. Everything seemed to be going swimmingly. Then, without warning, a gust of wind took it. I was on my back in a flash, being dragged across the highway and into the opposite lane. Fortunately, a tractor-trailer labouring up the hill posed the only threat, going slow enough to veer around my sprawling body.

So much for that bright idea, I thought angrily, disentangling myself from the muddle of cords and scrambling to my feet. I would have to come up with some other solution before the twelve-mile sheer descent of Colorado's 10,863-foot Wolf Creek Pass.

In Geary, I was told of an Indian pow-wow beginning the next day at Canton Lake, thirty miles north of Watonga. I was keen to find out more about these indigenous people, their links to the Earth, and what they ultimately valued. Did their concept of stewardship offer clues to a sustainable future for the world, I wondered?

Five miles short of Watonga, the day started to bleed from the western sky. I decided to camp early. A handsome hill with a slab top loomed in the failing light, the kind you'd expect to see in a Western with a mounted warrior at the edge. I tramped to the summit, whacking at the oak brush with my flag to scare away the rattlesnakes. Then I cooked and ate my usual fare of rice and tinned fish, meditated, and laid out my sleeping bag on a mattress of dry grass. Sleep came fitfully; coyotes yipped and barked close by. I awoke at first light shivering with cold, fresh from dreams of Jack London's frozen north, Alaska, wolves...

I reached Canton Lake mid-afternoon. Between the cottonwood trees, a raised podium with loud speakers faced an arena ringed by picnic chairs. The people gathered didn't exactly match my Hollywood-inspired notion of a pow-wow. Instead of feathered braves daubed in war paint stomping around a fire, I saw regular country folk in jeans, tee shirts, and cowboy hats slouching against flashy four-wheel drives, chatting.

The Canton Lake Pow-wow wasn't some Wild West Show laid on for the amusement of the public, I realized. It was very much a family affair. As the odd one out, I just stood there, clutching my skates self-consciously.

Not for long. A granddad in a tattered baseball cap ambled up and offered his hand.

"Where ya from?" he asked.

I told him.

"Well, while you're here, you're one of us." He had a soft, lilting voice, slow and deliberate. "Eat our food and consider yourself a part of our family. Cheyenne Arapahos are the friendliest people you'll ever meet."

He smiled, shook my hand again, and shuffled off to the podium to make an announcement.

"Who was that?" I asked a woman standing nearby.

"Clinton Young Bear. He's the chief."

Really? I thought. *I'd sooner have guessed he was the maintenance man…*

His plain speaking had impressed me, though, the words he chose carefully articulated, as if the *way* he expressed them carried more weight than the actual words themselves. He'd tailored his own personal use of language by way of direct, intuitive experience, assigning more importance to its underlying form than the external packaging.

"If I could have your attention for a minute." It was the voice of

Clinton Young Bear booming over the public address system. "I see Dolly Parton is in the crowd tonight. Oh no, I'm sorry, it's just a couple of bald rednecks sitting with their heads together."

A few people chuckled. Most groaned. The chief obviously had a reputation for cracking feeble jokes.

"There is, however, a young guy who's come all the way from England to be with us here today." Everyone turned and stared at me. "So why don't you go on over and talk to him, make him feel at home."

A woman with black pigtails immediately hauled me off to a trestle table heaped with home cooking: fried chicken, rice, baked potatoes, corn on the cob, and the Indian artery-clogging favourite, fry-bread.

"The chief's family always lays on the first meal," Louise Hamilton explained. "Tomorrow, it'll be another family's turn."

At dusk, the low pounding of drums started up, echoing off the cottonwood trees that flickered golden brown in the light of the campfires. The arena quickly filled with fifty or so dancers for the Intertribal, an opening dance for everyone. Men, women, and children, their costumes gaily decorated with beads, feathers, and brightly coloured tassels, danced in their own distinctive styles: hopping, shuffling, leaping, and spinning.

"It's all about personal expression," said Louise, who'd made her own buckskin dress by hand. "Each dancer tells a traditional story, and there are many ways to interpret them, as many as there are dancers. All of them are true."

Before joining in herself, she introduced me to a Cheyenne man in a black cowboy hat. Bill agreed to answer some more of my questions.

"We seek inner guidance from *Wakan Tanka*... the Great Spirit." Like Chief Young Bear, he spoke in a low, nasal rumble, and his skin was deeply engraved as if glacially etched. "Kids do it in their early teens as a Vision Quest... They go to a place of solitude, a cave maybe… take no food… a little water…"

He took long, awkward pauses between phrases, sometimes leaving them stranded in midair altogether.*

"They stay there for three or four days," he continued, "calming the mind from wandering thoughts… focusing their attention inward…"

I was struck by the familiarity of his words, mirroring my own experiences on the Atlantic.

"If they're lucky, a spirit guide will be revealed to them… an animal totem… giving guidance for the rest of their life… Could be a hawk like it was for Crazy Horse… or a wolf…"

I mentioned sleeping the previous night on the slab-topped hill— "Indian Hill," I'd named it in my journal—with the coyotes yipping nearby.

Bill nodded. "We call that the Red Hill… My people have always gone there to cry for a vision… seek solutions to difficult questions… or the right path when they go astray… Even when we get older, sometimes we need to go back to where we came from… the wilderness… to remind us of our true nature… and to better understand our responsibilities to the Earth and its people…"

Later, by the lakeside, I lay listening to the distant cadence of falsetto voices rising to a wavering pitch, the circular drum beating faster and faster, digesting all that I'd heard. *You should stay longer and learn more*, I told myself. But a visit to the Watonga Grade School beckoned in the morning, and I was already up against it to cross the Sierras before the first snows.

---

* "Conversation was never begun at once, nor in a hurried manner. No one was quick with a question, no matter how important, and no one was pressed for an answer. A pause giving time for thought was the truly courteous way of beginning and conducting a conversation. Silence was meaningful with the Lakota, and his granting a space of silence to the speech-maker and his own moment of silence before talking was done in the practise of true politeness and regard for the rule that 'thought comes before speech'." *Luther Standing Bear, Oglala Sioux Chief.*

I drifted off counting fireflies suspended in the watery darkness, their luminescent bodies blinking like the lanterns of faraway ships crossing a turbulent sea.

Dede's Hilltop Tavern, 11:45 pm

"HEY ENGLISH! I got another one. You know yer a redneck when yer family tree ain't got no forks."

I'd heard this joke before, but I was plastered, so I laughed anyway. "That's a good one, Wade!"

My new drinking pal beamed with pleasure. "An' how's about... You know yer a redneck when a cop pulls you over and sez, 'Got any I.D.?' An' you say, 'About what?'"

Describing himself as part German, Cheyenne Indian, and Swedish—"An' some coyote in there, too!" someone yelled across the bar—Wade was a self-avowed mutt, a true crossbreed. He also claimed to be full-blood redneck. In case anyone doubted the genealogical integrity of this claim, he bared the front of his tee shirt. It read: MY WORST DAY HUNTING IS BETTER THAN MY BEST DAY SHOPPING WITH THE WIFE.

I was in Oakwood, Oklahoma, a hole in the road 160 miles from the Kansas border. "Blink and you'll miss it," the folks in Watonga had said. Earlier, while filling my water bottles outside the service station where he worked, Wade had wandered over, yellow Scandinavian hair sticking out from under a greasy orange cap, and asked, "Whatcha doin' on them things?"

It was 6:00 pm. He was just getting off work pumping fuel. Would I like a beer?

After skating all day under the blistering Oklahoma sun, uphill, and into a headwind, I lost no time confiding in this stranger the answer to one of the longest-standing mysteries concerning the private lives of bears. That yes, they did indeed shit in the woods.

Dede's Hilltop Tavern could call its own shots when it came to customer service; it was the only watering hole for miles around. A sign above the kitchen declared, "This is not a Burger King. You don't get it *your* way. You get it *my* way. Or you don't get the doggone thing." Another above the bar read, "I don't give any shit. I don't take any shit. 'Cos I ain't in the shit business"—right next to a decree that any unattended children would be sold as slaves. A framed photograph showed one of the patrons grinning inanely, his arm thrust down the throat of a sixty-five-pound channel catfish, also grinning inanely.

If my intention had been to use rollerblades as a way of unmasking the raw underbelly of small-town America, then this was it. I'd hit the mother lode.

Sitting beside me at the bar, Wade remembered that it was his son's tenth birthday. I found a used skate wheel in my backpack, and scribbled a message around the rim in black marker. A ten-dollar bill was promptly slipped under my beer glass, and then the night really got going. Soon every upright soul in the joint was three sheets to the wind, and laying bets on a selection of fat, shiny cockroaches corralled in Dede's kitchen and pressed into roach derbies on the pool table.

By midnight, Wade was cross-eyed and tilting thirty degrees off the vertical. "Yer welcome to crash at my place tonight," he hiccuped. "I'm fixin' road kill breakfast in the mornin'."

Outside, he showed me what he meant. A deer lay dead in the back of his pickup, one of its hind legs broken.

"Found it by the side of the highway." Wade chuckled. "Sure hate to see good food go to waste!"

I nodded vaguely in agreement, although privately I wondered how long the carcass had been stewing in the heat.

Next, we were bumping along a dirt track towards his home.

"While we's out here," my host suddenly blurted, "why don' I give you a li'l tour of Oakwood, show you the main sites?"

I looked for any trace of irony in his face, but there was none. The first port of call was the trailer house where Wade was born. As we pulled up, the shoebox structure revealing itself in the headlights, his expression fell. All the windows had been smashed, and the walls covered in graffiti.

"Geez!" cried Wade. "Them goober kids, they'll vandalize anythin' historical."

Next up was the river he fished as a kid. After driving off-road for what seemed an eternity, we abandoned the truck and took off on foot into a snarl of willows. Wade assured me the river was close, but after half an hour of tripping over the recalcitrant willows and sprawling in cow shit, we were clearly lost. If we hadn't been hopelessly drunk, one of us might have thought to bring a flashlight. As it was, such presence of mind was a distant fantasy by this point. Wade pulled out his lighter, which not surprisingly turned out to be empty. He resorted to striking the flint, ruining our night vision in the process.

On we blundered, homing in on every cowpat in Oklahoma, it seemed, but no river. Finally, Wade stopped.

"Two things don't make a whole lotta sense here, English."

I was all ears. Oakwood, Oklahoma was never going to be the Pyramids or the Taj Mahal. Even so, the "main sites" had been a disappointment. I was tired and I longed for sleep.

"First, where that sonofabitchin river is."

"No shit, Wade. And the second?"

He laughed with hearty confidence. "How neither of us has got bit by a cottonmouth yet!"

I froze. Cottonmouths, also known as water moccasins, are deadly snakes found in and around watercourses in the American South.

"Maybe we can... continue the tour tomorrow?" I suggested nervously.

Forty minutes later, having stumbled across the truck by accident, we were rolling into Wade's front yard, a plot of scorched earth littered with the rusting remains of abandoned vehicles and prehistoric farming equipment.

"Make yourself at home," he slurred, falling through the front door and collapsing on a diseased-looking sofa. "'Cos no one else will."

And with that, my illustrious host passed out.

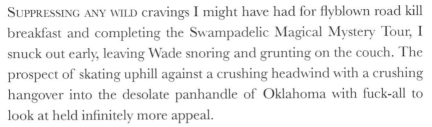

SUPPRESSING ANY WILD cravings I might have had for flyblown road kill breakfast and completing the Swampadelic Magical Mystery Tour, I snuck out early, leaving Wade snoring and grunting on the couch. The prospect of skating uphill against a crushing headwind with a crushing hangover into the desolate panhandle of Oklahoma with fuck-all to look at held infinitely more appeal.

North of Liberal, Kansas, the roads began zigzagging through a chequerboard of corn, alfalfa, and wheat fields. I became Pac-Man on wheels, travelling straight up or across the board, never diagonally. The tedium of linear trajectory wasn't helped by the homogenized surroundings. The endless irrigated green was like watching paint dry. I took to using the prairie cathedrals as psychological carrots to skate towards. These vast grain silos first appeared as tiny swellings on the treeless horizon, pushing incrementally skyward, revealing the curvature of the Earth in microscopic slow motion, until they towered hundreds of feet into the air with me skating ant-like beneath.

On the evening of September 7, I arrived at a Loaf 'N Jug convenience store on Highway 50, an east-west corridor taking me over the Rockies to California. Taking a seat at one of the tables inside, I laid out my now heavily taped US wall map and worked out where I was. The town of Syracuse was roughly equidistant between Fort Lauderdale and San Francisco, 2,274 miles in either direction.

Reaching the halfway point was a major milestone, I reminded myself. After all, not so many days and weeks ago I was sitting beside State Road 19 in Florida, blubbering like a baby, resolved to biking cross-country instead of skating. But celebrations were the last thing on my mind. My dwindling funds had reached crisis level. I counted out the remaining coins on the red tabletop.

Three dollars and ten cents...

The next town big enough to raise funds giving talks was Pueblo, 170 miles away. Skating sixty miles three days in a row wouldn't normally pose a problem, but a dollar-a-day wasn't much to buy in the way of food. I was weak with hunger as it was.

I picked out two packets of orange slices from the ninety-nine cent, two-for-one candy rack, and handed the money to the cashier.

"Which way ya headed?" She took my four quarters and popped them in the register. Now I was down to two dollars and eleven cents.

"San Francisco," I replied, and the talk inevitably turned to the expedition.

"Sounds like a helluvan' adventure!" The woman had a kind face. Her name was Nina. "Say, my dad's a teacher at the grade school here. Would you be interested in giving a quick talk to the kids t'morra?"

The answer, unfortunately, had to be a polite but firm "No." I'd already given a dozen free talks to summer camps, youth groups, and schools along the way. As broke as I was, I needed to prioritize. The earlier I got going in the morning, the better my chances of reaching Pueblo before running out of money completely.

"Okay," I agreed, immediately cursing my big mouth. I never had known how to say no.

After a freezing night on the concrete slab behind the store, balled up in my ultra-light sleeping bag, the "quick talk" ended up stretching to three one-hour presentations lasting well into the afternoon. I felt queasy with hunger by the time I stashed the box of slides in my backpack and prepared to leave. All I'd eaten in the last 24 hours was five orange slices—little more than sugar and colouring.

"Hey Jason, hold up there a minute!"

It was the principal, Mr Birch. "The teachers and kids did a little whip-round for your journey." He held out an envelope. "It's not very much I'm afraid, a little under a hundred dollars, but we hope it helps."

Hope it helps? From where I was standing, starving and destitute, he'd just handed me a winning lottery ticket. Now I had plenty of money to reach Pueblo. Maybe there was even enough to buy some cold weather gear? I needed a fleece jacket for the mountains, socks, sleeping mat, long johns...

Skating out of the schoolyard, a conversation I'd had with Steve and Stuart popped into my head. Completing the circumnavigation "without a pot to piss in," as Stuart frequently pointed out, was dependent upon several key factors, notably the kindness of strangers in lieu of proper funding, and bags of determination, adaptability, and resourcefulness on our parts. But perhaps most important of all was faith. Faith that a solution to our debts would eventually manifest itself if we kept going. Faith that the *means* to keep going would, at times, appear from sources we couldn't possibly foresee.

When the way ahead is clouded with uncertainty, the safety net is gone, and every iota of logic is howling at you to give it all up and go home, *that* is the time to push on regardless, surrendering to the free fall of not knowing. For the universe has an uncanny habit of responding to such blind leaps into the abyss, rising up to meet them halfway. All you have to do is keep an open mind, an open heart, and have faith. The rest is out of your hands.

TWO NIGHTS LATER I camped near Bent's Old Fort, a reconstructed nineteenth century adobe trading post for trappers and local Indian tribes. Now at an elevation of more than four thousand feet, the air was noticeably thinner, and the nights colder. I built a fire to keep warm, waking periodically to add more wood.

5:15 am. At first light I was up, teeth chattering as I strapped on my skates. It was eighty-seven miles to Pueblo, my longest day's skate yet. By evening, if all went well, I would be at the foot of the Rockies. Then, a brief layover, and the hard work would really begin: scaling the Continental Divide.

The day started well enough, a road kill cantaloupe supplying breakfast on the run. But as I pushed into the wide, fertile valley of the Arkansas River west of La Junta, the sky turned the colour of an oily rag, dark and foreboding. The distant Rockies, visible in the pre-dawn light as a set of baby teeth pushing up from the western horizon, disappeared behind a dust cloud of almost biblical proportions. Upon entering this opaque domain, the sweet mountain air turned to an ungodly stench, sour and acrid. Then I passed the cause of it: thousands of penned cattle, all churning around in their own shit, not a blade of grass in sight. A feedlot, I was later told, supplying America's insatiable demand for beef.

I'd already passed several of these plumping depots, albeit unwittingly, where yearling steers are artificially inflated from a winter pasture weight of nine hundred pounds to a portly fourteen hundred, before being shipped off to be slaughtered. Not long after these gut-churning encounters with the hormone-infusing, antibiotic-pumping, multi-billion-dollar cattle industry, I turned vegetarian.*

2:35 pm. I was cruising along at a fair clip on the hard shoulder

---

* Einstein's words further inspired me: "Nothing will benefit human health and increase the chances for survival of life on Earth as much as the evolution to a vegetarian diet."

when a rumble strip appeared out of nowhere. It was too late to stop, and an eighteen-wheeler thundering up behind made veering out of the way impossible. My 84 millimetre skate wheels fit the grooves perfectly, launching me into space. I landed heavily on my forearms, stripping off the newly formed skin from an earlier fall. Unleashing the usual litany of expletives, I clambered to my feet, plucked a large chunk of gravel from my right elbow, and pressed on.

Then it began to rain. This was open country with few trees offering shelter. The only option was to tough it out until the next town. *This is really starting to bite The Big One*, I thought, struggling to keep my balance on the slick tarmac. But if the conditions seemed harsh now, I was in for a surprise. The day's trials were only beginning.

A mile beyond Fowler, a blue sedan stopped ahead of me. An effeminate man in his early twenties rolled down the window. Was everything okay? I asked.

He looked at me sheepishly, and lisped, "I was just wondering if you'd like a blowjob?"

I choked. "I'm sorry. A *what?*"

"A blowjob."

"That's what I thought you said." I shook my head and turned to go. "Thanks, but no thanks."

"Oh please..."

I looked back at my would-be paramour. He looked anaemic, his eyes sunken in their sockets, colourless lips trembling.

My temper flared. "No! For *fuck's* sake— Listen, you can't just drive around the country offering blowjobs to random strangers. You're lucky I'm not a local. I'd have probably shot you by now!"

His lips quivered some more. "But you're not a local. *Please*, I just wanna give you a blowjob."

Then he burst into tears.

Un–Fucking–Believable, I thought. *Here I am, standing in the pouring rain, blood pouring down my arm, trying to explain to some weeping fruitcake why I don't want him to use my manhood as a toothpick.*

"Fuck this," I muttered, and skated away.

WEST OF FOWLER, gunmetal curtains of rain peeled back to reveal a stunning mackerel sky. The sun broke through mid-afternoon, and blankets of yellow butterflies thronged the steaming tarmac to sup at the dampness.

4:55 pm. With only an hour and a half of daylight remaining, Pueblo was still thirty-five miles away. On any other day, I would camp before the city limits, and knock out the remaining miles in the morning. But a special treat was in store, a simple pleasure I hadn't partaken of in a long time.

A bed.

In Lamar, shortly after crossing into Colorado, I'd met the Grett family whose daughter studied at the University of Southern Colorado in Pueblo. A phone call was made. The sofa bed in Jill's shared apartment reserved. Elmer, the proud father, showed me a photograph of his daughter and her roommate, Alexis. They were both stunners.

Summoning last reserves, I willed my weary legs on. By 6:40 pm, I was inside the city limits. *Only three miles to go…*

Another thunderstorm swept in from the south, torrential this time, rendering the surface unskatable. I joined a motorcyclist sheltering under a railway bridge. Together we watched the stream of rush hour traffic sluicing past on the dual carriageway, headlights flashing in the puddles.

6:50 pm. The rain let up enough for us both to continue. The air was fresh and vibrant, the smell of damp, musty earth saturating my lungs. I came to an on-ramp, waited for a break in traffic, and returned quickly to the safety of the hard shoulder. I remember seeing a footbridge up ahead, khaki-coloured bungalows set back from the road. I was humming the Merle Haggard song playing in a convenience store back in Fowler. A 55 mph sign took shape in the fading light. Then—

WHAM!!

The sense of force was incredible, a visceral, stomach-wrenching impact of freight train proportions. Bile heaved into my throat. I was on my back, staring up at the darkening sky. *What just happened?* My mind spun a loop. Had a wing mirror clipped me? Had some jackass driving past slapped the back of my head?

No pain, though. Can't be too serious…

I tried standing up, but something wasn't right. Looking down, I saw the gross distortion: my skates pointing backwards. Instead of my feet, I was standing on the stumps of my lower legs, tibias jammed in the dirt.

Horrified at the sight of porcelain-white bone poking through jagged flaps of skin, I fell backwards. Nausea rose up. Anger too. *Stupid fucking idiot,* I railed at myself. *Why didn't you stop earlier?* Then, a moment later, a wave of relief: *But I'm alive. Thank goodness I'm alive!*

I called out for help, but my cries were swallowed by the night. Again, stronger this time, screaming at the top of my lungs: *"Help! Someone, please, HELP!"* Grabbing the orange flag, I began frantically waving at the traffic. It remained indifferent. Nobody was stopping. I waved and screamed… waved and screamed…

Seconds turned into minutes. Then everything went dark.

THE EXPEDITION CONTINUES IN PART TWO:

THE SEED BURIED DEEP

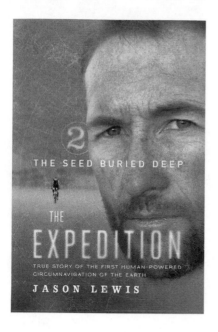

PART 2: *THE SEED BURIED DEEP*

When adventurer Jason Lewis regained consciousness beside a busy Colorado highway, lower limbs shattered by a hit and run driver, he knew he was lucky to be alive. But would he ever walk again, let alone finish crossing North America by inline skates?

So begins part two of *The Expedition*, a stirring saga of hope, determination, and the kindness of strangers as Jason, taken in by the people of Pueblo, spent nine months in rehabilitation, legs pieced together with metal rods, before returning to the spot he was run over, and continuing on.

Inspired by the journey, others sought to join, including a middle-aged mother-cum-schoolteacher yearning to see the world. For the expedition wasn't just a line on a map. *The real expedition was the seed buried deep in the heart of anyone who has ever dreamed of knowing what lies beyond their valley, and of embarking upon a grand adventure to find out…*

More at www.billyfishbooks.com

GLOSSARY OF NAUTICAL TERMS & BRITISH VERNACULAR

Aft	Towards the rear of a boat
Antipodal points	Pair of points diametrically opposite each other on the surface of a sphere, such as the Earth
Back garden	Backyard
Banger	Clunker. Also a sausage
Beam	Midpoint of a ship
Bidet	Automatic ass washer invented by the French
Bilge	Lowest compartment of a ship. Also, utter nonsense
Billy No Mates	Sad loser with no friends
Biscuit	Cookie
Blagger	Smooth-talking con artist
Bloke	Dude
Bloody Hell	Common expletive used in anger, shock, or surprise
Bollard	Short post used to divert traffic
Bollocks	Expletive. Also testicles
Bollocks to this	To hell with it
Bosun	Ship's officer in charge of crew and equipment
Bow (sounding like cow)	Front end of a boat
Breezeblock	Cinder block
Briny	The sea
Broach	Boat slewing side-on to wind and waves
Boxing Day	The day after Christmas
Bugger	Goddamnit
Buggered	Tired out, exhausted
Bugger off	Get lost
Buggery	Sodomy. Not a conservatory for bugs
Chalk and Cheese	Like night and day
Cheeky	Sassy

Circumnavigation	*A true circumnavigation of the world must pass through two points antipodean to each other*— Norris McWhirter, co-founder of the Guinness Book of Records, 1971
Cock-up	Snafu, or wake up call for a rooster
Crikey	Darn
Davy Jones's locker	Bottom of the sea, considered the grave for drowned sailors
Diddled	Cheated or swindled out of something
Dole	Welfare
Doss	Sleeping rough, outside or on someone's couch
Down tools	Walk off the job
Dustbin	Trash can
Faffing	Dicking around achieving absolutely nothing
Fag	Cigarette. Not to be confused with a homosexual
Flogging	Selling something, or masochistic clog dancing
Fore	Towards the front of a boat
Foredeck	Deck at the front of a boat
Fortnight	Two weeks
Froggies	Derogatory name English use for the French, referring to their penchant for *cuisses de grenouille*, a dish featuring frogs' legs
Gin Palace	Ostentatious pleasure craft
Girl's blouse	Sissy
Glaswegian	Native of Glasgow, Scotland
Great circle	Shortest distance between any two points on a sphere, esp. Earth
Gunwales	Upper edge of a ship, formerly a support for cannon
Halyard	Rope used for raising and lowering a sail on a yacht
How's-yer-father	Sneaky sex. Not to be confused with Who's yer daddy
Knackered	See Buggered
Knots	Nautical miles per hour

Larder	Pantry
Lavatory	Bathroom
Lay-by	Turnout
Lee side	Sheltered side (as of a boat) away from the wind
Lock-in	When pub customers get to continue drinking after closing time
Loo roll	Toilet paper roll
Lorry	Semi truck
Mate	Buddy. Commonly used by Australian, New Zealand and British men when they can't remember each other's names
Money for old rope	Easy money
Nick	Illegal alternative to buying. Also jail
Offing	Area of the sea closest to the horizon
Plonk	Poor quality wine
Po-faced	Face like a pug licking a stinging nettle
Porridge	Oatmeal
Port	Left side of a boat looking towards the bow
Punter	Ill-informed customer likely to be taken advantage of
Quarter	Either side of a ship behind the midpoint
Quay	Dock
Quid	British pound sterling
Rosbifs	Derogatory name French use for the English, referring to their tendency to turn bright red from over exposure to the sun
Roundabout	Traffic circle
Row (sounding like cow)	Shouting match. Not to be confused with row, as in rowing a boat
Sextant	Instrument used in navigation, not fornication
Shite	Shit. Also worthless drivel
Skeg	Fin beneath a boat's stern
Skip	Dumpster
Sod	Jerk
Sod it	Forget it, I've had enough
Sod's Law	Murphy's Law

Spanner	Wrench
Squat	Abandoned building typically inhabited by homeless people
Starboard	Right side of a boat looking towards the bow
Stern	Rear end of a boat
Taking the piss	Tease. Not to be confused with taking *a* piss
Tiller	Lever on top of a rudder used for steering
Topknot	Knot of hair on someone's head or tuft of feathers on a bird
Torch	Flashlight
Tot	Small measure of alcoholic drink
Transom	Stern section of a square-ended boat
Wangle	Contrive something
Wank	Masturbate
Wanker	Total bastard
Wedding Tackle	Penis

CONVERSIONS

1 pound sterling = 1.60 US dollars (approximate)
1 nautical mile = 1.151 statute miles
1 statute mile = 1.609 kilometres